Advanced
Adobe® Photoshop® CC
Digital Classroom™

for Design Professionals

Jennifer Smith and the AGI Creative Team

WILEY | AGI

Advanced Adobe® Photoshop® CC Digital Classroom™ for Design Professionals

Published by
John Wiley & Sons, Inc.
10475 Crosspoint Blvd.
Indianapolis, IN 46256

Copyright © 2014 by John Wiley & Sons, Inc., Indianapolis, Indiana
Published simultaneously in Canada
ISBN: 978-1-118-12414-7
Manufactured in the United States of America
10 9 8 7 6 5 4 3 2 1

For general information on our other products and services or to obtain technical support, please contact our Customer Care Department within the U.S. at (877) 762-2974, outside the U.S. at (317) 572-3993 or fax (317) 572-4002.

Wiley publishes in a variety of print and electronic formats and by print-on-demand. Some material included with standard print versions of this book may not be included in e-books or in print-on-demand. If this book refers to media such as a CD or DVD that is not included in the version you purchased, you may download this material after registering your book at www.digitalclassroombooks.com/CC/AdvPhotoshop. For more information about Wiley products, visit www.wiley.com.

Please report any errors by sending a message to errata@agitraining.com

Library of Congress Control Number: 2012937912

Credits

Additional Writing
Bill Carberry, Joel Howe, Paul Sinclair

President, American Graphics Institute and Digital Classroom Series Publisher
Christopher Smith

Executive Editor
Jody Lefevere

Technical Editors
Haziel Olivera, Lauren Mickol

Editor
Karla E. Melendez

Editorial Director
Robyn Siesky

Business Manager
Amy Knies

Senior Marketing Manager
Sandy Smith

Vice President and Executive Group Publisher
Richard Swadley

Vice President and Executive Publisher
Barry Pruett

Senior Project Coordinator
Katherine Crocker

Project Manager
Cheri White

Graphics and Production Specialist
Jason Miranda, Spoke & Wheel

Media Development Project Supervisor
Chris Leavey

Proofreading
Karla E. Melendez

Indexing
Michael Ferreira

Stock Photography
iStockPhoto.com

About the Authors

Jennifer Smith is a designer, educator, and author. She has authored more than 20 books on digital design and creative software tools. She provides consulting and training services across a wide range of industries, including working with software developers, magazine publishers, catalog and online retailers, as well as some of the biggest names in fashion, apparel, and footwear design. When not writing and consulting you'll often find her delivering professional development workshops for colleges and universities.

Jennifer also works extensively in the field of web usability and user experience design. Jennifer works alongside application developers and web developers to create engaging and authentic experiences for users on mobile devices, tablets, and traditional computers. She has twice been named a Most Valuable Professional by Microsoft for her work in user experience (UX), user interface (UI) design fields, and her leadership in educating users on how to integrate design and development skills.

Jennifer Smith's books on Photoshop, Illustrator, and the Creative Suite tools include the *Photoshop Digital Classroom*, the *Illustrator Digital Classroom*, and the *Adobe Creative Suite for Dummies*, all published by Wiley. She has also authored *Wireframing and Prototyping with Expression Blend & Sketchflow*.

Jennifer is the cofounder of the American Graphics Institute (AGI). You can find her blog and contact her at *JenniferSmith.com* and follow her on Twitter @jsmithers.

The **AGI Creative Team** is composed of Adobe Certified Experts and Instructors from AGI. The AGI Creative Team has authored more than 25 Digital Classroom books and has created many of Adobe's official training guides. The AGI Creative Team works with many of the world's most prominent companies, helping them use creative software to communicate more effectively and creatively. They work with design, creative, and marketing teams around the world, delivering private customized training programs, while also teaching regularly scheduled classes at AGI's locations. The AGI Creative Team is available for professional development sessions at companies, schools, and universities. Get more information at *agitraining.com*.

Acknowledgments

Thanks to our many friends at Adobe Systems, Inc. who made this book possible and assisted with questions and feedback during the writing process. To the many clients of AGI who have helped us better understand how they use Photoshop and provided us with many of the tips and suggestions found in this book. A special thanks to the instructional team at AGI for their input and assistance in the review process and for making this book such a team effort.

Thanks iStockPhoto (*iStockPhoto.com*) for their permission to use exclusive photographers for images throughout the *Advanced Adobe Photoshop CC Digital Classroom for Design Professionals* book.

Register your Digital Classroom book for exclusive benefits

Registered owners receive access to:

 The most current lesson files

 Technical resources and customer support

 Notifications of updates

 Online access to video tutorials

 Downloadable lesson files

 Samples from other Digital Classroom books

Register at *DigitalClassroomBooks.com/CC/AdvPhotoshop*

DigitalClassroom

Register your book today at
DigitalClassroomBooks.com/CC/AdvPhotoshop

Contents

Starting up

Lesson 1: Introduction to Advanced Navigational Features

Lesson 2: Taking Advantage of Adobe Bridge

Lesson 3: Advanced Selection Techniques

Lesson 4: The Pen Tool: Beyond the Primer

Lesson 5: Color Correcting like a Pro

Lesson 6: Painting and Retouching

Lesson 7: Creating Compositions

Lesson 8: Creating Special Effects

Lesson 9: Advanced Use of the Vector Tools

Lesson 10: Creating Images for the Web and Application Design

Lesson 11: Zipping it up with Automation Tools

Lesson 12: Using Photoshop for 3D

Starting up

About Advanced Adobe® Photoshop® CC Digital Classroom™ for Design Professionals

The *Advanced Adobe® Photoshop® CC Digital Classroom for Design Professionals* provides a broad foundation of essential Photoshop skills. It is the perfect way to learn Photoshop if you are just starting out with the software, upgrading from a previous version, or if you have never received formal training—even if you have been using Photoshop for years. The *Advanced Adobe Photoshop CC Digital Classroom* provides designers and creative professionals the knowledge they need to create exciting images, efficiently retouch photos, and create compelling special effects. This book helps you extend your Photoshop skills beyond the basics and teaches you advanced uses for masking, color correction, and special effects. Whether you use Photoshop for color correction and retouching of images, creating digital artwork, designing web pages, or creating advertisements, the *Advanced Adobe Photoshop CC Digital Classroom* takes your Photoshop skills to the next level. This book is the follow-up to the best-selling introductory Photoshop book: *Photoshop Digital Classroom*.

The *Advanced Adobe Photoshop CC Digital Classroom for Design Professionals* helps you get up-and-running right away. You can work through all the lessons in this book, or complete only specific lessons. Each lesson includes detailed, step-by-step instructions, along with lesson files, useful background information, and video tutorials on the included DVD—it is like having your own expert instructor guiding you through each lesson while you work at your own pace. This book includes 12 self-paced lessons that let you discover essential skills, explore new features, and understand capabilities that will save you time. You'll be productive right away with real-world exercises and simple explanations. The *Advanced Adobe Photoshop CC Digital Classroom* lessons are developed by the same team of Photoshop experts who have created many official training titles for Adobe Systems.

Prerequisites

Before you start the *Advanced Adobe Photoshop CC Digital Classroom for Design Professionals* lessons, you should have experience using the tools in Photoshop. You should understand how to access tools and panels as well as how to use the workspace effectively.

Before starting the lessons files in the *Advanced Adobe Photoshop CC Digital Classroom*, make sure you have installed Adobe Photoshop CC. The software is sold as part of the Creative Cloud and is not included with this book. Find more information about the Creative Cloud at *www.adobe.com/CreativeCloud*. You can use the free 30-day trial version of Adobe Photoshop CC available at the *adobe.com* website, subject to the terms of its license agreement.

System requirements

Before starting the lessons in the *Advanced Photoshop CC Digital Classroom*, make sure that your computer is equipped for running Adobe Photoshop CC. The minimum system requirements for your computer to effectively use the software are listed below and you can find the most current system requirements at *http://www.adobe.com/products/photoshop/tech-specs.html.*

Windows

- Intel® Pentium® 4 or AMD Athlon® 64 processor (2 GHz or faster)
- Microsoft® Windows® 7 with Service Pack 1 or Windows 8 with Service Pack 1
- 1 GB of RAM
- 2.5 GB of available hard-disk space for installation; additional free space required during installation (cannot install on removable flash storage devices)
- 1024 × 768 display (1280 × 800 recommended) with 16-bit color and 256 MB of VRAM (512 MB of VRAM recommended for 3D features)
- OpenGL 2.0–capable system
- Internet connection and registration are necessary for required software activation, membership validation, and access to online services.

Mac OS

- Multicore Intel processor with 64-bit support
- Mac OS X v10.7 (64 bit) or v10.8 (64 bit)
- 1 GB of RAM
- 3.2 GB of available hard-disk space for installation; additional free space required during installation (cannot install on a volume that uses a case-sensitive file system or on removable flash storage devices)
- 1024 × 768 display (1280 × 800 recommended) with 16-bit color and 256 MB of VRAM (512 MB of VRAM recommended for 3D features)
- OpenGL 2.0–capable system
- Internet connection and registration are necessary for required software activation, membership validation, and access to online services.

Starting Adobe Photoshop CC

As with most software, Adobe Photoshop CC is launched by locating the application in your Programs folder (Windows) or Applications folder (Mac OS). If you are not familiar with starting the program, follow these steps to start the Adobe Photoshop CC application:

Windows

1   Choose Start > All Programs > Adobe Photoshop CC.
2   If a Welcome Screen appears, you can close it.

Mac OS

1   Open the Applications folder, and then open the Adobe Photoshop CC folder.

2   Double-click the Adobe Photoshop CC application icon.

3   If a Welcome Screen appears, you can close it.

Menus and commands are identified throughout the book by using the greater-than symbol (>). For example, the command to print a document appears as File > Print.

Resetting Adobe Photoshop CC preferences

When you start Adobe Photoshop, it remembers certain settings along with the configuration of the workspace from the last time you used the application. It is important that you start each lesson using the default settings so that you do not see unexpected results when working with the lessons in this book. The method described in the following steps restores Photoshop back to the original setting. If you have made changes to your Colors Settings and want to maintain them, follow the steps in the section, "Steps to reset default settings, but keep color settings."

Steps to reset Adobe Photoshop CC preferences

1   If Photoshop is open, choose File > Exit (Windows) or Photoshop > Quit (Mac OS).

2   Press and hold the Ctrl+Alt+Shift keys (Windows) or Command+Option+Shift keys (Mac OS) simultaneously while launching Adobe Photoshop CC.

3   A dialog box appears verifying that you want to delete the Adobe Photoshop settings file. Release the keys, and then click OK.

Steps to reset default settings, but keep color settings

As you reset your preferences to the default settings, you might want to keep your color settings. This is important if you have created specific color settings, or work in a color-calibrated environment.

Use the following steps to reset your Adobe Photoshop CC preferences and save your color settings.

1   Launch Adobe Photoshop CC.

2   Choose Edit > Color Settings, and then click the Save button. The Save dialog box opens. Enter an appropriate name for your color settings, such as the date. Leave the destination and format unchanged, then click the Save button. The Color Settings Comment dialog box opens.

3   In the Color Settings Comment dialog box, enter a description for the color settings you are saving and then click OK. Click OK again in the Color Settings dialog box to close it. You have saved your color settings so they can be accessed again in the future.

4   Choose File > Quit to exit Adobe Photoshop CC.

5   Press and hold the Ctrl+Alt+Shift keys (Windows) or Command+Option+Shift keys (Mac OS) simultaneously when launching Adobe Photoshop CC. A dialog box appears verifying that you want to delete the Adobe Photoshop settings file. Release the keys and then click OK.

6   After Adobe Photoshop CC launches, choose Edit > Color Settings. The Color Settings dialog box appears.

7   From the Settings drop-down menu, choose your saved color settings file. Click OK. Your color settings are restored.

A note about color warnings

Depending on the configuration of your Color Settings, there might be times you receive a Missing Profile or Embedded Profile Mismatch warning. If you do receive Missing Profile or Embedded Profile Mismatch warnings, choose the Assign working option, or Convert document's colors to the working space. The working space is determined by what you have assigned in the Color Settings dialog box. Color Settings are discussed in more detail in Lesson 5, "Color Correcting like a Pro" and in Lesson 6, "Painting and Retouching."

Missing color profile.

Mismatched color profile.

Access lesson files and videos any time

Register your book at *www.digitalclassroombooks.com/CC/AdvPhotoshop* to gain access to your lesson files on any computer you own, or to watch the videos on any Internet-connected computer, tablet, or smartphone. You can continue your learning anywhere you have an Internet connection. This provides you access to lesson files and videos even if you misplace your DVD.

Checking for updated lesson files

Make sure you have the most up-to-date lesson files and learn about any updates to your *Advanced Photoshop CC Digital Classroom for Design Professionals* book by registering your book at *www.digitalclassroombooks.com/CC/AdvPhotoshop.*

Loading lesson files

The *Advanced Photoshop CC Digital Classroom for Design Professionals* DVD includes files that accompany the exercises for each of the lessons. You can copy the entire lessons folder from the supplied DVD to your hard drive, or copy only the lesson folders for the individual lessons you want to complete.

For each lesson in the book, the files are referenced by file name. The exact location of each file on your computer is not used, since you might have placed the files in a unique location on your hard drive. We suggest placing the lesson files in the My Documents folder (Windows), at the top level of your hard drive (Mac OS), or on your desktop for easy access.

Copying the lesson files to your hard drive

1 Insert the *Advanced Photoshop CC Digital Classroom* DVD supplied with this book.

2 On your computer desktop, navigate to the DVD and locate the folder named advpslessons.

3 You can install all the files, or just specific lesson files. Do one of the following:

   • Install all lesson files by dragging the advpslessons folder to your hard drive.

   • Install only some of the files by creating a new folder on your hard drive named advpslessons. Open the advpslessons folder on the supplied DVD, select the lesson you want to complete, and drag the folder(s) to the advpslessons folder you created on your hard drive.

Unlocking Mac OS files

Macintosh users might need to unlock the files after copying them from the accompanying disc. This only applies to Mac OS computers and is because the Mac OS might view files that are copied from a DVD or CD as being locked for writing.

If you are a Mac OS user and have difficulty saving over the existing files in this book, you can use these instructions to update the lesson files as you work on them and add new files to the lessons folder.

Note that you only need to follow these instructions if you are unable to save over the existing lesson files, or if you are unable to save files into the lesson folder.

1   After copying the files to your computer, click once to select the advpslessons folder, then choose File > Get Info from within the Finder (not Photoshop).

2   In the advpslessons info window, click the triangle to the left of Sharing and Permissions to reveal the details of this section.

3   In the Sharing and Permissions section, click the lock icon, if necessary, in the lower-right corner so you can make changes to the permissions.

4   Click to select a specific user or select everyone, then change the Privileges section to Read & Write.

5   Click the lock icon to prevent further changes, and then close the window.

Working with the video tutorials

Your *Advanced Adobe Photoshop CC Digital Classroom for Design Professionals* DVD comes with video tutorials developed by the authors to help you understand the concepts explored in each lesson. Each tutorial is approximately five minutes long and demonstrates and explains the concepts and features covered in the lesson.

The videos are designed to supplement your understanding of the material in the chapter. We have selected exercises and examples that we feel will be most useful to you. You might want to view the entire video for each lesson before you begin that lesson. Additionally, at certain points in a lesson, you will encounter the DVD icon. The icon, with appropriate lesson number, indicates that an overview of the exercise being described can be found in the accompanying video.

DVD video icon.

Setting up for viewing the video tutorials

The DVD included with this book includes video tutorials for each lesson. Although you can view the lessons on your computer directly from the DVD, we recommend copying the folder labeled videos from the *Advanced Photoshop CC Digital Classroom for Design Professionals* DVD to your hard drive.

Copying the video tutorials to your hard drive

1   Insert the *Advanced Photoshop CC Digital Classroom* DVD supplied with this book.

2   On your computer desktop, navigate to the DVD and locate the folder named videos.

3   Drag the videos folder to a location on your hard drive.

Viewing the video tutorials with the Adobe Flash Player

The videos on the *Advanced Photoshop CC Digital Classroom* DVD are saved in the Flash projector format. A Flash projector file wraps the Digital Classroom video player and the Adobe Flash Player in an executable file (.exe for Windows or .app for Mac OS). Note that the extension (on both platforms) might not always be visible. Projector files allow the Flash content to be deployed on your system without the need for a browser or prior stand-alone player installation.

Playing the video tutorials

1   On your computer, navigate to the videos folder you copied to your hard drive from the DVD. Playing the videos directly from the DVD could result in poor quality playback.

2   Open the videos folder and double-click the Flash file named PLAY_ADVPSCCvideos to view the video tutorials.

3   After the Flash player launches, click the Play button to view the videos.

    The Flash Player has a simple user interface that allows you to control the viewing experience, including stopping, pausing, playing, and restarting the video. You can also rewind or fast-forward, and adjust the playback volume.

A. Go to beginning. B. Play/Pause. C. Fast-forward/rewind. D. Stop. E. Volume Off/On. F. Volume control.

Playback volume is also affected by the settings in your operating system. Be certain to adjust the sound volume for your computer, in addition to the sound controls in the Player window.

Additional resources

The Digital Classroom series goes beyond the training books. You can continue your learning online, with training videos, at seminars and conferences, and in-person training events.

On-demand video training from the authors

Comprehensive video training from the authors are available at *DigitalClassroom.com*. Find complete video training along with thousands of video tutorials covering Photoshop and related Creative Cloud apps along with digital versions of the Digital Classroom book series. Learn more at *DigitalClassroom.com*.

Training from the Authors

The authors are available for professional development training workshops for schools and companies. They also teach classes at American Graphics Institute, including training classes and online workshops. Visit *agitraining.com* for more information about Digital Classroom author-led training classes or workshops.

Additional Adobe Creative Cloud Books

Expand your knowledge of creative software applications with the Digital Classroom book series. Books are available for most creative software applications as well as web design and development tools and technologies. Learn more at *DigitalClassroomBooks.com*

Seminars and conferences

The authors of the Digital Classroom seminar series frequently conduct in-person seminars and speak at conferences, including the annual CRE8 Conference. Learn more at *agitraining.com* and *CRE8summit.com*.

Resources for educators

Visit *digitalclassroombooks.com* to access resources for educators, including instructors' guides for incorporating Digital Classroom into your curriculum.

What you'll learn in this lesson:

- Navigation tips and tricks
- Creating custom shortcuts
- Changing menu Items
- Saving custom workspaces

Introduction to Advanced Navigational Features

Photoshop's advanced tools help you build realistic imagery quickly and professionally. In this lesson, you find out how to use the workspace to work as efficiently as possible.

Starting up

Before starting, make sure that your tools and panels are consistent by resetting your preferences. See "Resetting Adobe Photoshop CC preferences" in the Starting up section of this book.

You will work with several files from the advps01lessons folder in this lesson. Make sure that you have loaded the advpslessons folder onto your hard drive from the supplied DVD. (For more detailed instructions, see "Loading lesson files" in the Starting up section of this book.)

See Lesson 1 in action!

Use the accompanying video to gain a better understanding of how to use some of the features shown in this lesson. You can find the video tutorial for this lesson on the included DVD.

Speeding up your navigation process

In this lesson, you will work with a layered file composition to help you to discover workspace tips and tricks you can use to create graphics more efficiently.

1 Choose File > Browse in Bridge to open Adobe Bridge.

2 Navigate to the advps01lessons folder contained within the advpslessons folder on your computer, and double-click **advps0101.psd** to open it in Photoshop. An image of a woman in a city appears. You won't do a lot with this file, but it will help you learn how you can work more efficiently in the Photoshop CC workspace.

The working file for this lesson.

3 Choose File > Save As and name this file **advps0101_work.psd**; choose to save it in the advps01lessons folder. Keep it open for the next part of the lesson. If a Photoshop Format Options dialog box appears, click OK.

Navigational tips

Navigating your image quickly for efficient retouching is critical. The following chart shows frequently used keyboard shortcuts that will be used throughout this book.

FUNCTION	WINDOWS SHORTCUT	MAC OS SHORTCUT
Fit on Screen	Ctrl+0 (zero)	Command+0 (zero)
Zoom In	Ctrl+"+" (plus sign—don't include the quotation marks)	Command+"+" (plus sign—don't include the quotation marks)
Zoom In	Ctrl+Spacebar+click	Command+Spacebar+click
Zoom Out	Ctrl+"-" (minus sign—don't include the quotation marks)	Command+"-" (minus sign—don't include the quotation marks)
Zoom Out	Alt+Spacebar+click	Option+Spacebar+click
100% size	Ctrl+1	Command+1

You can double-click the Zoom tool to view your image at actual size.

Practice with Zooming controls

In this part of the lesson, you have an opportunity to try some helpful navigational tips.

1   With the **advps0101_work.psd** image open, press Ctrl+0 (zero) (Windows) or Command+0 (Mac OS) to fit the image in the window. This keyboard shortcut works in most Adobe applications and is a quick and easy way to see the entire image, illustration, or page.

2   Press the Tab key. Notice that the tools and the panels disappear.

3   Press Ctrl+0 (zero) (Windows) or Command+0 (zero) (Mac OS) again to see that, now that the panels are gone, the image can take up even more screen space.

4   Press Tab again and the tools and other panels reappear. The Tab key is a toggle switch that will hide or show panels and tools, as long as you are not in the active Type tool.

As you position your cursor over various tools, you'll see a letter to the right of the tool name in the tooltip. This letter is the keyboard shortcut that you can use to access that tool. You could, in fact, work with the Tools panel closed and still have access to all the tools.

5   Press Ctrl/Command+"+" (plus sign) or Ctrl/Command+"-" (minus sign) to see how you can easily zoom in and out of your image.

6   When you are finished practicing with the Zooming shortcuts, press Ctrl/Command+0 (zero).

Dynamic zooming and panning

To zoom and pan more dynamically into your image, you can use one of two main methods: a combination of keyboard shortcuts while clicking and dragging; or the Navigator panel. In this part of the lesson, you will start with the keyboard shortcuts.

1   To use the dynamic method of zooming in with a keyboard shortcut, you need to disable the Scrubby Zoom feature in the Zoom tool. Do this by selecting the Zoom tool and unchecking the Scrubby Zoom button in the Options bar at the top of the workspace.

The keyboard shortcuts you are about to use work when you have any of the tools selected, so you should select a tool other than the Zoom tool to try the shortcut.

2   Choose any other tool in the Tools panel other than the Zoom tool.

3   Ctrl+Spacebar+click (Windows) or Command+Spacebar+click (Mac OS) and drag over the bright light that appears in the upper-center of the image area. Notice that a marquee appears; when you release the tool, the zoom result is based upon the marquee position and the size of the marquee that you create.

Click and drag to zoom into a specific area.   *The resulting view.*

4   To dynamically pan, press and hold the spacebar; your cursor becomes a hand (🖐). Pressing and holding the spacebar allows you to click and push the image around and reposition the view. This helps you avoid using the scrollbars when navigating an image.

5   Press Ctrl/Command+0 (zero) to go back to the fit in screen view.

With the Zoom tool selected, you can click and drag a marquee area to control the zoom.

Using the Navigator panel

You can also use the Navigator panel to control the view in Photoshop. The Navigator panel has been available in many versions and is a helpful tool for keeping an eye on an entire composition while zooming into specific areas.

1 Select Windows > Navigator; the Navigator panel opens.

The Navigator panel shows the entire image. A red box (called the proxy view) in the image area of the Navigator panel identifies the area currently being viewed in the active window. You can change the proxy view by clicking and dragging the red box to other locations in the Navigator panel. The view percentage—how much of the whole image you're currently able to see—is shown in the lower-left corner of the Navigator panel. To zoom in or out, you can either type in a new percentage or use the slider at the bottom of the panel.

2 Unpin the Navigator panel from the dock by clicking the tab of the panel and dragging it out of the dock.

Click and drag the lower-right corner of the panel to make it larger.

3 Click and drag the lower-left corner of the Navigator panel to make it larger (just enough to see the details of the image).

4 Press Ctrl/Command+(Plus sign) a few times to zoom in anywhere in the image. This displays a proxy view (red rectangle) in your Navigator panel.

5 Move the cursor over the proxy view (red rectangle). Your pointer turns into the Hand tool (🖐). Drag the proxy view to the top-left corner. This allows you to quickly scroll to that part of the image. Next, you will control your zoom with a key modifier.

Move the proxy view (red box) to navigate your image.

6 Press and hold the Ctrl (Windows) key or the Command (Mac OS) key while hovering with your cursor over the Navigator panel; your cursor becomes the Zoom tool (⊕). Click and drag over the head of the girl in the image. When you release, the exact location of the region you created is enlarged to the maximum level.

Use Ctrl/Command to zoom.

7 Press Ctrl+0 (Windows) or Command+0 (Mac OS) to fit the image to the screen.

8 Select Window > Workspace > Reset Essentials to return to the default workspace.

Maximizing productivity with screen modes

Now that you can quickly zoom in and out of your image, you will discover how to take advantage of screen modes. You have a choice of three screen modes in which to work. Screen modes control how much space your current image occupies on your screen, and whether you can see other Photoshop documents as well. The Standard Screen mode is the default screen mode when you open Photoshop for the first time. It displays an image on a black background and also provides a flexible work area for dealing with panels.

By changing the screen modes, you can locate over-extended anchor points and select more accurately up to the edge of your image. Changing modes can also help you present your image to clients in a clean workspace.

1 With the **advps0101_work.psd** image file open, press **F** to cycle to the next screen mode, which is Full Screen Mode With Menu Bar. This view surrounds the image out to the edge of the work area with a neutral gray (even behind the docking area) and displays only one image at a time, without tabs and centered within the work area. You can access additional open images by choosing the image name from the bottom of the Window menu.

You can also change your screen mode by clicking and holding the Change Screen Mode button in the Tools panel, and selecting Full Screen Mode With Menu Bar.

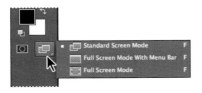

The Change Screen Mode button accessed in Tools panel.

Notice that the black background area (pasteboard) now extends to fill your entire screen and that your image is centered within that area. One of the benefits of working in this mode is that it provides more area when working on images.

The Full Screen mode with Menu bar.

2   Press **F** again to see the last screen mode, Full Screen Mode.

Full Screen mode.

This is Full Screen mode. This mode allows you to show others your document full-screen with no distracting screen elements. All menus and panels are hidden automatically in this mode; however, they are still accessible by hovering the cursor over the area where the panels normally reside. The panels temporarily reappear for easy access. If you'd like to see the panels while in this mode, press the Tab key to display and hide them.

3   Press the **F** key once to cycle back into Standard Screen mode. Stay in this mode throughout this lesson.

Creating your own keyboard shortcuts

As you become more skilled, you might choose to use keyboard shortcuts for virtually every task. However, there are some functions in Photoshop that do not have assigned keyboard shortcuts. Fortunately, you can create your own using the Keyboard Shortcuts menu item. In this part of the lesson, you'll assign new keyboard shortcuts to menu items that are popular, but lack a keyboard shortcut.

1 With the **advps0101_work.psd** image still open, choose Edit > Keyboard Shortcuts; the Keyboard Shortcuts dialog box appears.

Note that you start with the Photoshop Defaults. This shows the keyboard shortcuts that are available without customization. The Shortcuts For menu indicates that the shortcuts you see are for the Application Menus; these are the menu items that appear at the top of your Photoshop Workspace.

2 Click the arrow to the left of Edit to expose the menu items that typically appear under the Edit menu. Scroll down and select the Check Spelling item; the text field under Shortcut becomes active.

Type a new shortcut into the text field, but choose an option that does not conflict with an existing shortcut.

If you do type a conflicting shortcut, a warning sign will appear (⚠), along with a message indicating where that keyboard shortcut is presently being used. To use a conflicting shortcut, click the Accept and Go to Conflict button; to find a keyboard shortcut not being used, select Undo Changes.

You can add your own shortcut.

Photoshop does not allow a keyboard shortcut to be used for two different commands. When you click the Accept and Go to Conflict button, the conflicting shortcut will be applied to your selected command, but you will need to change the shortcut for the command that originally had that shortcut. For example, the keyboard shortcut Ctrl+1 is used to show an image at 100% size. If you were to assign this command to allow the spellchecker to appear, and clicked the Accept and Go to conflict button, Photoshop would apply the Ctrl+1 keyboard shortcut to the appearance of the spellchecker, but would make you change (or remove) the keyboard shortcut to show an image at 100% size to something else.

Some keyboard shortcuts cannot be changed. These are the shortcuts used for specific functionality where the keyboard shortcut must remain consistent, for example, in the use of channels.

Some keyboard shortcuts cannot be changed.

3 Press the F10 key to allow the spellchecker to appear when the F10 key is pressed.

4 Click Accept, and then click OK.

Using your new shortcut

You will now use the new shortcut you created. For this exercise, a layer with a misspelled word was created and hidden.

1 With the **advps0101_work.psd** file still open, click the visibility icon to view the layers named "This is mispelled" and "She stood and watched...".

2 Press F10. The Spellchecker dialog box appears, alerting you to the fact that a misspelled word has been found. The word is "mispelled" and a suggestion is presented.

3 Click Change to use the first suggestion. Click OK to close the Spell check complete alert window. Click OK to close the Spell Checker dialog box.

4 You can turn off the visibility of the "This is mispelled" layer.

5 Choose File > Save and keep the file open for the next part of this lesson.

Saving and summarizing your keyboard shortcuts

You can save and summarize your keyboard shortcuts to share them with others, or print a list for reference.

1 With the **advps0101_work.psd** image still open, choose Edit > Keyboard Shortcuts. Notice the two icons and the trash icon to the right of the Set name, at the top of the Keyboard Shortcuts and Menus dialog box.

2 Click the Create new set (📥) icon. When the Save dialog box appears, type **My Shortcuts** into the Save As text field; keep the location in Keyboard Shortcuts, and click Save.

The Keyboard Shortcuts folder is located in your Photoshop Application folder, in the Presets folder. You could also choose to copy your shortcut set to a server to share with other users; they would then copy the set to their Presets > Keyboard Shortcuts folder.

Next, you will save a copy of your shortcuts in a text format for reference.

Choose to save your set with a custom name.

3 Click the Summarize button; the Save dialog box appears. The name My Shortcuts is already in the Save As dialog box. Choose to save to your advps01lessons folder and click OK (Windows) or Save (Mac OS). The My Shortcuts file is a text file that you can open using TextEdit, Notepad, Microsoft Word, or other applications that can read text.

4 Click OK to close the Keyboard Shortcuts and Menus dialog box.

You can save or print your shortcuts for reference.

Editing the menu items

In this section, you are going to customize your workspace even further by removing some of the items that you do not need in your menu. This will help keep your workspace much more streamlined.

1 Make sure that you still have the **advps0101_work.psd** file open, and then choose Edit > Menus. The same Keyboard Shortcuts and Menus dialog box appears, but this time the Menus tab is forward.

2 Select the arrow to the left of Edit. There are many items in the Edit menu that an advanced user might not need, such as Cut and Copy.

3 Click the visibility icon (👁) to turn off the Cut and Copy menu items.

Note that you can save a set of Menu items as well, just as you would Keyboard Shortcuts, by clicking the Create new set (📥) icon to the right of the Set drop-down menu. You won't be doing it for this lesson.

4 Click OK, and then go to the Edit menu. Notice that Cut and Copy menu items are no longer available in the list of Edit menu items.

If you choose to see all menu items, scroll to the bottom of the menu item and select Show All Menu Items. This temporarily brings back the hidden menu items.

Using Photoshop Extras

There are many extra items that you can show to help you to make more precise adjustments to your images. You can access many of these accessed individually through keyboard shortcuts, or you can turn them all off and on with the Show Extras menu item.

You will start by taking advantage of some precision features that will help you to build more professional layouts and designs in Photoshop.

Using rulers and guides

You can easily access rulers and change them to any increment you want, or even to show the rule in percentage amounts.

1   With the **advps0101_work.psd** file still open, press Ctrl+R (Windows) or Command+R (Mac OS). Pressing Ctrl/Command R shows and hides the ruler.

The default for the North American version is that the rulers are in inch increments. You can change this by right-clicking the horizontal or vertical ruler and selecting the measurement you want to use.

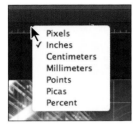

*You can show rulers and change
the measurement increment.*

*You can also access the increments by selecting Edit > Preferences > Units &Rulers (Windows)
or Photoshop > Preferences > Unites & Rulers (Mac OS).*

2 Right-click the horizontal ruler (top) and select Percent.

You will now create guides.

3 Click the top ruler and drag. Note that a guide follows your cursor out of the ruler position. Continue dragging the guide down until you reach approximately 75% percent of the way down.

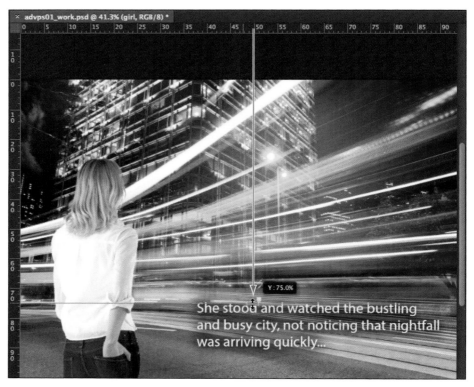

Drag a guide down from the top to about the 75% mark.

4 Press Ctrl+: (colon) (Windows) or Command+: (colon) (Mac OS) to turn off and on the visibility of the guides.

You can delete a guide by selecting the Move tool (✛), and then clicking and dragging the guide back into the ruler. You can eliminate all guides by selecting View > Clear Guides.

Using the Grid

Given the amount of website and application layouts that developers usually do in Photoshop, the grid is an extremely useful and helpful tool. In this part of the lesson, you will discover how to set up your gird preferences and adjust content to align to the grid.

1   Choose Edit > Preferences > Guides, Grids and Slices (Windows) or Photoshop > Preferences > Guides, Grid and Slices (Mac OS). The Preferences dialog box appears. Here you can change the colors of the guides and grid. Slices are used when creating HTML or CSS tables and you can change the color of those items in this dialog box as well. In this section, you will focus only on the grid.

2   Select the Grid Color drop-down menu, and choose Custom.

3   When the Color Picker appears, choose a dark grey color. Our example uses R:**120**, G:**120**, B:**120**. Click OK to close the Color Picker.

Change the Grid color to a dark grey.

4   Change the Gridline Every to a value of **20** and the increment to Pixels. Leave the subdivisions at 4. This gives you 5 px. units to align your items.

5   Click OK to close the Preferences dialog box.

6 Press Ctrl+" (double-quote) (Windows) or Command+" (double-quote) (Mac OS) to turn on the grids.

There are several toggle keyboard shortcuts that you can use when you only want to show some of the Extras.

FUNCTION	WINDOWS	MAC OS
Show Rulers	Ctrl+R	Command+R
Show Grid	Ctrl+"	Command+"
Show Guides	Ctrl+:	Command+:

Using the guides and grids to align text

You will now use the guide and grid to align the text.

1 With the **advps0101_work.psd** image still open, select the Move tool (▸₊), and then tun on the visibility and select the text layer named She stood and watch...

2 Press and hold the Ctrl+Spacebar (Windows) or Command+Spacebar (Mac OS), then click and drag to zoom into the left side of the text.

Press and hold Ctrl/Command+Spacebar and click and drag to zoom in.

3   Using the Move tool, click and drag the text upwards until the baseline of the first line of text falls on the guide.

You can also nudge the text upwards by pressing the up arrow (⇧) several times.

Align the baseline of the text on the Guideline.

When building a clean layout it is suggested that you use a grid to align items in your design. In the next steps, you will align the moon using the grid lines.

4   Turn on the visibility of the Moon layer by clicking the Visibility icon, and then select that layer.

5   Make sure that you are on the Move tool; use the left and right arrow keys to nudge the moon so the right edges are 2 units (or eight subdivisions) away from the start of the text.

6   Use the up and down arrows to nudge the moon so it also rests on the guide.

7   When you are finished lining these items up, press Ctrl+0 (zero) (Windows) or Command+0 (zero) (Mac OS).

Turning off and on Extras

To align items in this image, you worked with one of the Extra options available in Photoshop, but there are many more Extra options available to you. You can activate these individually, or turn them off and on at once.

1 Press Ctrl/Command+" (double-quote) to turn off the grid, press Ctrl/Command+" (double-quote) again to turn the grid back on.

2 To turn off and on the Extras, Choose View Extras. The View Extras is a toggle check box: if you select it, a checkmark appears indicating that the Extras are visible. If you click it to clear the check box, the Extras become invisible.

3 Choose View Show > All to see the applicable extra features appear, such as slices, grids, and layer edges. Many of these are helpful, especially when building designs for applications and websites, but not all of them are needed at the same time.

4 Choose View > Show > Show Extras Options; a dialog box appears with about 17 items. These items are the Extras that you can turn off or on when you trigger the option to show Extras. You can leave them all checked for this lesson.

5 Choose View > Extras to turn off the visibility of all the Extras.

6 Choose File > Save to save this file. Keep this file open for the next part of the lesson.

Customizing your panels

You can customize the panels you want to see. The panels you use depend upon your workflow and the type of work that you produce. In this part of the lesson, you will arrange panels that are already visible and choose to show an additional panel. As you progress through this book, you might decide to make changes to panels that you have arranged, and that is fine, since you can always update your saved workspace, which you will cover in the next section.

Finding the panels you want

As an advanced user, you have been accessing panels for most of your tasks in Photoshop. You might have some favorites that you want to have readily available, and you might also have some panels that you choose to never use.

The easiest way to find a panel is by selecting it from the Windows menu, since you can find all the panels at this location, including the Tools, Application frame, and the Tools option. You can also keep most of your favorite panels open and collapse them to icons, or arrange them into logical groups.

1 With the **advps0101_work.psd** image still open, choose Windows > Workspace > Reset Essentials so you can follow along with this exercise.

2 Right-click the tab of the Color panel; in the contextual menu that appears, choose Collapse to Icons. All the panels collapse to icons.

3   Select the Swatches panel to make it appear. Select Adjustments; notice that the Swatches panel goes away and only the Adjustments panel is visible. You can keep valuable space open in your workspace by only showing the panels that you are actively using.

4   Right-click any of the collapsed panels and select Expand Panels from the context menu. All the panels expand.

5   Click the tab of the Layers panel and drag it out to the left of the dock, essentially dragging it out into the workspace area.

6   Click the tab of Paths and drag the panel over to the Layers panel; the Paths panel is now docked to the Layers panel, forming a custom panel group.

You can customize all your panels by creating your own groups. Find the panels you don't need and close them by clicking the "X", or by choosing Close from the Panel menu in the upper-right area of the panel.

Now that you have some customization in the keyboard shortcuts, menus, and panels, you will save all these items in one custom workspace.

Customizing workspaces

Throughout this lesson, you have seen how you can improve the workspace by changing shortcuts, menus and panels. In this section, you will learn how to save time by creating a new custom workspace. This way, you can quickly reset preferences in later lessons and still be able to work with your saved workspace.

1   Choose Windows > Workspace > New Workspace; the New Workspace dialog box appears. Note that you have the opportunity to save your panel organization and any preferences that you set for Keyboard Shortcuts and Menus.

2   Name your workspace **My Workspace** and select the Keyboard Shortcuts and Menus check boxes. Click Save when you're done.

You can save your workspace preferences.

3   Choose Windows > Workspace > Essentials to make sure you are back to the default workspace.

4 Test your saved workspace by selecting Windows > Workspace > My Workspace.

Now that you have saved your own workspace, you might want to investigate some of the other saved workspaces that are part of Photoshop. You can choose from workspaces that were created for typography, 3D, photography, and more. Access these workspaces by selecting Windows > Workspace.

In this lesson, you discovered how to set up your workspace to help you work more efficiently in Photoshop. Look for additional features, such as using presets and setting other preferences, throughout this book to help you to improve your workflow even more.

You will keep this workspace since you need it for the lessons in this book. Once you're done with this book, you can choose to delete a custom workspace by selecting Window > Workspace > Delete Workspace. You can also select the workspace you no longer need and press Delete. Note that you cannot delete the default workspaces.

Self study

Practice taking an existing workspace and customizing it to your needs. Load the Typography workspace and customize the menu by removing the following items from the Edit menu: Fade; Copy Merged; Paste; Paste Special; and Clear. Save this new workspace as **My Typography** Workspace.

Review

Questions

1 How do you show menu items that have had their visibility turned off using the Keyboard Shortcuts feature?

2 Name one method you can use to change the increments of the ruler.

3 What is the keyboard shortcut for hiding and showing the grid?

4 How do you save a workspace?

5 Can you delete a workspace?

Answers

1 When you choose a menu that has invisible menu items, you can select Show All Menu Items from the bottom of the menu to make the menu items visible.

2 Here are two methods you can use to change the increments of a ruler in Photoshop:

- You can right-click the horizontal or vertical ruler; then, from the context menu that appears, select the increment you want to use.

- You can also choose Edit > Preferences > Units & Rulers (Windows) or Photoshop > Preferences > Units & Rulers (Mac OS).

3 To hide or show your grid, press Ctrl/Command+" (double-quote).

4 You can save your workspace by clicking the Workspace button in the Application bar and choosing Save Workspace.

5 Yes, you can delete a workspace by clicking the Workspace button in the Application bar and choosing Delete Workspace. Note that you cannot delete any of the default workspaces.

Lesson 2

What you'll learn in this lesson:

- Changing the Bridge workspace
- Finding and searching
- Building metadata tables
- Performing batch actions

Taking Advantage of Adobe Bridge

Adobe Bridge is the command center for your Creative Cloud applications and offers tools that allow you to sort, search, and batch common tasks. In this lesson, you will go beyond using Adobe Bridge as a method for previewing thumbnails of your images and explore its functionality.

Starting up

You will work with several files from the advps02lessons folder in this lesson. Make sure that you have loaded the advpslessons folder onto your hard drive from the supplied DVD. For more detailed instructions, see "Loading lesson files" in the Starting up section of this book.

See Lesson 2 in action!

Use the accompanying video to gain a better understanding of how to use some of the features shown in this lesson. You can find the video tutorial for this lesson on the included DVD.

1   Choose File > Browse in Bridge to open Adobe Bridge.

2   Navigate to the advps02lessons folder, and open it so that the thumbnail images appear in the Content panel in Adobe Bridge.

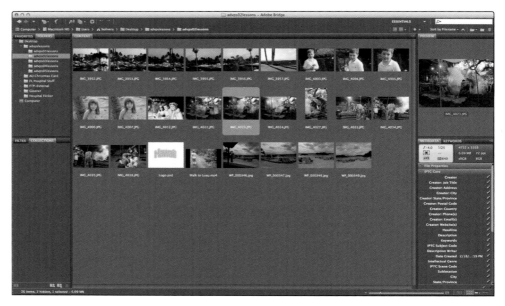

The content of the advps02lessons folder.

Why use Adobe Bridge

Bridge can help you locate files in less time when you need them. You can also preview your images quickly and find information such as the date the image was created, modified, and more. In this lesson, you will work in Adobe Bridge, create metadata templates, and discover other time-saving search features.

Bridge as a file browser

You can choose to use Adobe Bridge as a replacement for your own directory system. By selecting File > Browse in Bridge from most of the Adobe applications, you can navigate and preview your files before opening them in the application of your choice.

Sometimes, double-clicking to open a file in Adobe Bridge might open it in a different application than expected. This can happen if you are working in generic file formats such as .jpg, .png .or gif. To avoid this problem, you can right-click (Windows) or Ctrl+click (Mac OS) the image, and choose Open With to select the appropriate application.

Changing the view of Adobe Bridge

In this section, you'll adjust the workspace in Adobe Bridge to customize it to fit your needs. Changing Adobe Bridge (by adjusting the look and feel), can help you focus on the task at hand, and make it easier to find the right images when needed. Before starting, you will make sure that you are in the default view for Adobe Bridge.

1   Make sure you are in the Essentials workspace by selecting the Essentials button located in the upper-right area of the Bridge workspace. In this view, you see standard thumbnails and panels that include:

- **Favorites**: your standard system favorites appear here, such as your Computer, Documents, Pictures and more. You can also add your own folders here to make them easily accessible.

- **Folders**: represents your directory system and all the folders that it contains.

- **Filter**: allows you to filter the images you see in the content frame based on file type, keywords, date created, camera settings, and more.

- **Preview**: provides a preview of your file. You can play movies in this Preview panel, and navigate through pages of an InDesign file.

- **Metadata**: shows the associated metadata that automatically comes from your digital camera (EXIF). You can also enter your own metadata.

- **Keywords**: shows any keywords that have been applied. You can also add your own.

2   Click the Click to Lock to Thumbnail Grid button (▦) in the lower-right corner of the Bridge workspace. The images are organized into a grid.

3   Now click the View content as Thumbnails (▦) to see only thumbnail images.

4   Experiment with changing the size of the thumbnails by using the slider to the left of the preview buttons. You can also change the thumbnail size by pressing Ctrl+"+" (plus sign without the quotes) or Ctrl+"–" (minus sign without the quotes) (Windows) or Command+"+" (plus sign without the quotes) or Command+"–" (minus sign without the quotes) (Mac OS).

5 Now click the View content as details button (⬛️) to see a thumbnail and details about the creation date, last modified date, and file size.

Changing the view of Adobe Bridge.

6 Choose the View Content as List button (☰) to see the contents consolidated into a neat list that you can easily scroll through.

7 When you are finished experimenting with the preview modes select the preview mode you prefer or select the View content as thumbnails button.

Workspaces

In this lesson, you will work in the Essentials workspace, which you can change by selecting one of the following four options from the upper-right area of the Bridge workspace.

- **Essentials**: offers the default settings, which include the Preview, Metadata, and Keywords panels.

- **Filmstrip**: eliminates the panels on the right side of the workspace and presents one large thumbnail with a horizontal scroll for the thumbnails at the bottom.

- **Metadata**: shows the Metadata panel prominently on the left and a small thumbnail along with text view of any associated metadata.

- **Keywords**: shows the Keyword panel prominently on the left, along with thumbnail and metadata.

- **Preview:** Shows thumbnails on the left and a preview of the selected file on the right.

- **Light Table:** Expands the content pane across the entire workspace.

- **Folders:** Displays folders on the left, and the contents of the selected folder on the right.

Using folders in Adobe Bridge

Adobe Bridge is used for more than just navigating your file system. You can use Bridge to manage and organize folders and files.

1   Click the tab of the Folders panel in the upper-left corner of the Bridge window to make sure it is forward. Then click the arrow to the left of Desktop to display its contents. (If you are on the Mac OS, you can click Desktop to show its contents.)

2   Click Computer to reveal its contents in the center pane of the Bridge window. Continue double-clicking items, or clicking the arrows to the left of the folder names in the Folder panel to reveal their contents.

You can use Adobe Bridge to navigate your entire system, much as you would by using your computer's directory system.

Managing folders

Adobe Bridge is a great tool for organizing folders and files. To reorder items on your computer, all you need to do is drag and drop those items. You can create folders, move folders, move files from one folder to another, and copy files and folders to other locations; any organizing task that you can perform on the computer you can also perform in Adobe Bridge. This is a great way to help keep volumes of images organized for easy accessibility, as well as easy searching. One advantage of using Adobe Bridge for these tasks is that you have bigger and better previews of images, PDF files, and movies, with much more information about those files at your fingertips.

3   Click Desktop in the Folders panel to reveal its contents again.

4   Click advps02lessons to view its contents. You'll now add a new folder into that lessons folder.

5   Click the Create a New Folder icon (📁) in the upper-right corner of the Bridge window to create a new untitled folder. Type the name **Hotel**.

Creating a new folder in advps02lessons using Bridge.

You can use Adobe Bridge to organize images. Since you can see a preview of each file, you can more easily rename them, as well as relocate them to more appropriate locations in your directory system. In the next step, you will move files from one folder to the new Hotel folder you have just created.

6   Click once on the image named **IMG_3952.jpg**, and then Shift+click the image named **IMG_3956**. All the images in-between are selected.

Remember that you can easily reduce and enlarge the size of your thumbnails by pressing Ctrl++ (plus sign) or Ctrl+- (minus sign) (Windows) or Command++ (plus sign) or Command+- (minus sign) (Mac OS).

7 Click and drag the selected images to the Hotel folder. When the folder becomes highlighted, release the mouse. The files have now been moved into that folder.

You can select multiple images and organize folders directly in Adobe Bridge.

8 Double-click the Hotel folder to view its contents. The files that you moved appear.

9 Click advps02lessons in the file path bar at the top to return to that folder content.

Making a Favorite

One of the many great features in Bridge is that you can designate a frequently-used folder as a Favorite, allowing you to quickly and easily access it from the Favorites panel. This is extremely helpful, especially when the folders that you access frequently are stored deep in your file hierarchy.

1 Select the Favorites panel in the upper-left corner of the Bridge window to bring it to the front. In the list of Favorites, click Desktop. Double-click the advps02lessons folder to see the vacation images. Since the Hotel folder is going to be used again in this lesson, you'll make it a Favorite.

2   Place your cursor over the Hotel folder in the center pane (Content), and click and drag it to the location on the Favorites panel that says Drag Favorites Here, or underneath the last folder. When you see a horizontal line appear and your cursor shows a plus sign (⊞), release the mouse. On the Mac OS, you will see a circle with a plus sign. The folder is now displayed as a Favorite.

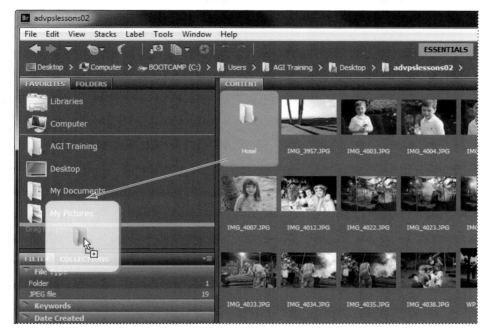

Drag a folder to the bottom of the Favorites panel to make it easier to locate.

3   Click the Hotel folder shown in the Favorites panel to view its contents. Note that creating a Favorite creates a shortcut for quick access to a folder; it does not copy the folder and its contents.

4   When you are finished looking inside the Hotel folder, click the Go back arrow, in the upper-left area, to return to the advps02lessons folder.

If your Favorite is created from a folder on an external hard drive or server, you will need to have the hard drive or server mounted in order to access it.

Stacking your images

You can organize your files by stacking them as a group to consolidate a selection of images into one thumbnail in the Adobe Bridge Content panel.

1   Select the image of the boy named **IMG_4003.JPG**, and then Shift+click the image named **IMG_4005.png**. The three images of the boy are selected.

2   Right-click any one of the three images and select Stack > Group as Stack from the context menu. The three images are consolidated together.

3   Click the number "3" in the upper-left area of the stack thumbnail to reveal the entire stack.

4   Click the "3" again to consolidate the stack.

You can quickly stack images with keyboard shortcuts. The following table lists these shortcuts.

FUNCTION	SHORTCUT WINDOWS	SHORTCUT MAC OS
Group as Stack	Ctrl+G	Command+G
Ungroup from Stack	Ctrl+Shift+G	Command+Shift+G
Close Stack	Ctrl+Left Arrow	Command+ Left Arrow
Expand All Stacks	Ctrl+Alt+Right Arrow	Command+Option+Right Arrow

Creating and locating metadata

Metadata is information that can be stored with images. This information travels with the file and makes it easy to search for and identify the file. In this section, you are going to find out how to locate and create metadata.

1   Make sure that you are viewing the contents of the advps02lessons folder in the center pane of Adobe Bridge. If not, navigate to that folder now.

2   Choose Window > Workspace > Reset Standard Workspaces. This ensures that you are in the Essentials view and that all the default panels for Adobe Bridge are visible. Alternatively, you can click Essentials in the Application bar at the top-right of the Bridge workspace. You might need to maximize your Bridge window after you reset the workspace.

Note that if you click the arrow to the right of the workspace presets, you can choose other workspaces, and even save your own custom workspace.

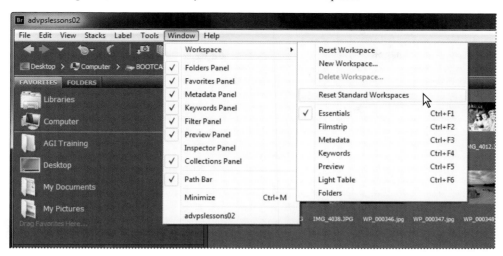

Resetting the workspace using the Workspace drop-down menu.

3   Click once on **IMG_4012.jpg**, and look for the Metadata and Keywords panels in the lower-right area of the Adobe Bridge workspace.

4   If the Metadata panel is not visible, click the Metadata panel tab. In this panel, you see the image data that is stored with the file. Take a few moments to scroll through the data and view the information that was imported from the digital camera that was used to take the photo.

Click and drag the bar to the left of the Metadata panel farther to the left if you need to open up the window.

5   If necessary, click the arrow to the left of IPTC Core to reveal its contents. IPTC Core is the schema for XMP that provides a smooth and explicit transfer of metadata. Adobe's Extensible Metadata Platform (XMP) is a labeling technology that allows you to embed data about a file, known as metadata, into the file itself. With XMP, desktop applications and back-end publishing systems gain a common method for capturing and sharing valuable metadata.

On the right side of this list, notice a series of pencil icons. The pencil icons indicate that you can enter information in these fields. Some of the information about the creator has already been included, such as the creator's name and his location. You will add additional information.

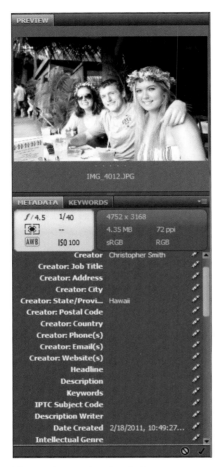

The Metadata panel can be edited.

If a file is locked, you won't be able to edit or add metadata information to it. Make sure that you are not working directly from the DVD, and then right-click the file (in Adobe Bridge) and choose Reveal in Explorer (Windows) or Reveal in Finder (Mac OS). In Windows, right-click the file, choose Properties, and click to clear the Read-only check box; in Mac OS, right-click the file, choose Get Info, then change the Ownership (Sharing) and Permissions to Read and Write.

6 Scroll down until you can see Description Writer, and click the pencil next to it. All editable fields are highlighted, and a cursor appears in the Description Writer field.

7 Type **Student**.

8 Scroll up to locate the Description text field. Click the Pencil icon to the right and type **Kona Village luau**, to add a description for the image.

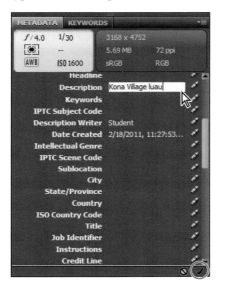

Reveal the IPTC contents and enter metadata information.

9 Click the Apply button (✓), located in the bottom-right corner of the Metadata panel, to apply your changes. You have now edited metadata that is attached to the image; this information will appear whenever someone opens your image in Bridge or views the image information in Adobe Photoshop using File > File Info.

Using keywords

Keywords can reduce the time it takes to find an image on a computer by using logical words to help users locate images more quickly.

1 With the same **IMG_4012.jpg** image still open, click the Keywords tab, which appears behind the Metadata panel. A list of commonly used keywords appears.

2 Click the New Keyword button (+) at the bottom of the Keywords panel. Type **luau** into the active text box, and then press Enter (Windows) or Return (Mac OS).

3 Select the check box to the left of the luau keyword. This adds the luau keyword to the selected image.

4 With the *luau* keyword still selected, click the New Sub Keyword button (⬚). Type **family** into the active text field, and then press Enter (Windows) or Return (Mac OS).

5 Select the check box to the left of the family keyword. You have now assigned a keyword and a sub-keyword to the **IMG_4012.jpg** image.

6 Select the luau keyword, and then click the New Keyword button (+) at the bottom of the Keywords panel; a blank text field appears. Type **faces** and press Enter (Windows) or Return (Mac OS). Then select the check box next to faces to assign the keyword to this image.

7 Right-click (Windows) or Ctrl+click (Mac OS) on the faces keyword, and choose the option Rename. When the text box becomes highlighted, type **smiles**, press Enter (Windows) or Return (Mac OS). Make sure the smiles check box remains selected.

*A. New Sub Keyword. **B.** New Keyword.*
C. Delete Keyword.

You can also enter information directly into the image by opening the image in Adobe Photoshop, and then choosing File > File Info. The categories that appear on the top include Description, Camera Data, IPTC, and IPTC Extension, among others. Once you enter this information into the File Info dialog box, the information is visible in Adobe Bridge.

Creating a Metadata Template

Once you have added metadata to an image, you can easily apply it to other images by creating a metadata template. In this exercise, you'll apply the metadata template from the **IMG_4012.jpg** image to some others in the same folder.

1 Make sure that **IMG_4012.jpg** is selected in Adobe Bridge.

2 Choose Tools > Create Metadata Template. The Create Metadata Template window appears.

3 In the Template Name text field (at the top), type **Hawaiian luau**.

In the Create Metadata Template window, you can choose the information that you want to build into a template. In this exercise, you will choose information that already exists in the selected file, but you could add or edit additional information.

4 Select the checkboxes to the left of the following categories: Creator, Creator: State/Province, Description, Keywords, Description Writer, Date Created, and then click Save.

Select a file and check the information you want to save into a metadata template.

You have just saved a template. Next, you will apply it to the other two sunset images in this folder.

5 Press Ctrl+A (Windows) or Command+A (Mac OS) to select all the images in this folder.

6 Choose Tools > Replace Metadata and select Hawaiian luau. Note that you can also choose Append Metadata if you want to keep existing metadata. You might receive a message stating that you cannot change all the metadata. If the message appears, it is because the changes you made will not activate the metadata in the Hotel folder. Click Yes to close the message box.

The same metadata has now been added to all the images at once.

acks Label [Tools] Window Help	
Batch Rename...	Ctrl+Shift+R
Create Metadata Template...	
Edit Metadata Template	▶
Append Metadata	▶ Hawaiian luau
Replace Metadata	▶
Cache	▶
Photoshop	▶

Choose the metadata template you want to use to add metadata to an image or images.

Searching for files using Adobe Bridge

Find the files that you want quickly and easily by using the Search tools built directly into Adobe Bridge, and taking advantage of the Filter panel.

Setting up unique keywords

For the purpose of practicing search, you will apply unique keywords to a couple of your images.

1 Ungroup the Stack group that you created earlier by selecting the Stack and then pressing Ctrl+Shift+G (Windows) or Command+Shift+G (Mac OS).

Unstack the images of the boy.

2 Select the image named **IMG_4005.jpg**, and then Shift+click **IMG_4006.jpg** to select both images.

3 In the Keywords panel, click the New Keyword button (+) at the bottom of the panel.

4 Type **children**, and then press Enter or Return.

5 Select the check box to the left of the children keyword to activate that keyword.

You can leave those images selected and move on to the next exercise.

Searching by name or keyword

Using the Find dialog box in Adobe Bridge, you can narrow your criteria down to make it easy to find your files when needed.

1 Make sure that you are still viewing the content in the advps02lessons folder.

2 Choose Edit > Find, or use the keyboard shortcut Ctrl+F (Windows) or Command+F (Mac OS). The Find dialog box appears.

3 Select Keywords from the Criteria drop-down menu, and type **children** into the third text field (replacing *Enter Text*.)

Notice that you can choose to include subfolders. This can speed up your search time if you are not sure where your files might be located.

4 Press Enter (Windows) or Return (Mac OS). All the images that you applied the Metadata template appear.

Search your folders using the tools built right into Adobe Bridge.

5 Clear the search by clicking the X icon (✖) to the right of the New Search icon at the top of the results pane.

You can clear the search by clicking the "X".

Using the Filter panel

You can use the Filter panel to easily locate files. Using the Filter panel, you can look at attributes such as file type, keywords, and date created or modified, to narrow down the files that appear in the content window of Adobe Bridge.

1 Make sure that you are still viewing the content of the advps02lessons folder. Notice that the Filter panel collects the information from the active folder, indicating the keywords that are being used, as well as modification dates and more.

2 Click the arrow next to Keywords in the Filter panel, and select children from the list. Notice that only images with the keyword children applied are visible. Click children again to deselect it and view all the images.

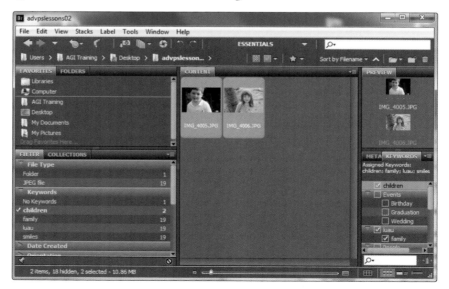

Find files quickly by selecting different criteria in the Filters panel.

3 Click the Clear filter button (⊘) in the lower-right area of the Filter panel to turn off any filters.

4 Experiment with investigating file types as well. Only file types that exist in the selected folder appear in the list. If you are looking for an Adobe Illustrator file, you might see that there are none located in this folder, but you will see an MP4 file that you can select and preview right in Adobe Bridge.

You can select File Types from the Filter panel to locate them easily.

5 Again, click the Clear filter button (⊘) in the lower-right area of the Filter panel to turn off any filters.

Using Adobe Bridge for automation

Adobe Bridge provides many tools to help you automate tasks. In this section, you will learn how to access and take advantage of some of these features.

Batch renaming your files

You might have noticed that in the advps02lessons folder there are many files that are generically named. These images were imported directly from a digital camera, and instead of changing the names, we have opted to change them simultaneously using the batch rename feature in Adobe Bridge.

1   Make sure that you are viewing the contents of the advps02lessons folder in Adobe Bridge.

2   Choose Edit > Select All, or press Ctrl+A (Windows) or Command+A (Mac OS.) All the images are selected. Don't worry if the Hotel folder is selected; the files inside will not be affected.

3   Choose Tools > Batch Rename. The Batch Rename dialog box appears.

In this instance, we want a simple uncomplicated name. If you look in the Preview section at the bottom of the Batch Rename dialog box, you can see that the Current filename and New filename are pretty long strings of text and numbers. You will simplify this by eliminating some of text from the filenames.

4   In the New Filenames section, type **Hawaii_** in the text field to the right of default criteria of Text.

5   In the Sequence Number row, verify that it is set to Two Digits.

6   Confirm that the sequence number is starting at 1. You can start it anywhere if you are adding additional images to a folder later.

7   If there is any other criteria, click the Minus sign button (−) (Remove this text from the file names) to remove them. The New filename in the Preview section becomes significantly shorter.

You can change multiple files names simultaneously in Adobe Bridge.

If you look in the Preview section at the bottom of the dialog box, you can see that the new filename is a very simple **Hawaii_01.jpg** now. Click the Rename button. All the selected files automatically have their name changed.

Select the naming Presets.   *The results.*

Saving time with the Image Processor

If you process many images, you can stay right in Adobe Bridge. In this part of the lesson, you take advantage of the Image Processor feature in Adobe Bridge, but you can discover more automated features in Lesson 11, "Zipping it up with Automation Tools." In this part of the lesson, you'll select the images in the Hotel folder, and convert them to low quality .jpgs, as well as reduce their overall size. This capability can be a huge time saver when processing images for websites or other applications.

1   In Adobe Bridge, double-click the Hotel folder to reveal the four images that you dragged in earlier.

2   Select Tools > Photoshop > Image Processor; the Image Processor dialog box appears.

If you do not have a Photoshop submenu under the Tools menu item, you might need to reinstall Adobe Bridge, since it would not have recognized your Photoshop installation.

3   In the Image Processor dialog box, select the radio button to the left of the greyed out Select Folder in Step 2. This will allow you to create a new folder on the Desktop to save your processed images into.

4   Click the Select Folder button, and in the Choose Folder dialog box that appears, pick a destination folder by navigating to the Desktop and clicking Make New Folder. Name the new folder **Optimized**, and click OK.

Choose Folder
Pick a destination folder

> ▷ 🖳 AGI Training
> ▷ 🖳 Computer
> ▷ 🖳 Network
> ▷ 🖳 Control Panel
> 🖳 Recycle Bin
> ▷ 🖳 advpslessons02
> 🖳 avsps02_images
> ▷ 🖳 desktop_items
> 🖳 Optimized

Folder: Optimized

[Make New Folder]   [OK]   [Cancel]

Choose to create a new folder for your processed images.

5   In the File Type section, choose Save as JPEG; if the quality is not at 5, select that now.

6   Check Resize to Fit and enter these values W: **250**, H: **167**. Note that you could also run additional actions if you had already created them. You will discover how to create actions in Lesson 10, "Creating Images for the Web and Application Design."

7   Enter the Copyright information **Student**.

Loading and saving settings

Once you establish a good set of Image Processor settings, you can re-use them. Do this by saving the Image Processor settings as an XML file. To save your settings, select the Save button and store your settings in your preferred location. You can share these settings with others, or just use them yourself by selecting Load, and then navigating to the saved settings.

8   Leave all other settings the same and click Run. The images are processed and sent to the Optimized folder on your desktop.

Load Files into Photoshop Layers

In this next section, you'll practice one of the most useful automated features in Adobe Bridge: loading files as Photoshop layers into one image. With this feature, you can select multiple files and open them all at once as a layered image file.

1   Return to the advps02lessons folder and use the Ctrl/Command key to click and select the **Hawaii_01.JPG**, the **Hawaii_02.JPG**, and the **Hawaii_16.JPG** file.

Select these three image files.

2   Choose Tools > Photoshop > Load Files into Photoshop Layers; the action starts to run in Photoshop. Once the action is complete, you'll see an Untitled file appear in Photoshop. If you take a look at the Layers panel, you'll see that there are three layers, appropriately named with the files names. You will now complete the composition in a few easy steps.

3   Click and drag the **Hawaii_16.psd** text layer to the top of the layers stack. Use the Move tool (✛) to reposition the Hawaii text to the right side of the image area.

4   Select the **Hawaii_01.JPG** layer and click Add layer mask button at the bottom of the Layers panel.

5 Select the Gradient tool ( ), and then click and drag from the right side of the image area to the left. When you are on a mask, this allows the image to fade out. You will learn more about masks in Lesson 7, "Creating Compositions."

Create a gradient on the layer mask to fade the image.

6 Choose File > Save and save this file as **advps0202**; leave it in the Photoshop (PSD) format, navigate to the advps02lessons folder, and click Save.

7 Choose File > Close to close this file and return to the Adobe Bridge.

Correcting images right from Adobe Bridge

In this section, you will learn how to make simultaneous corrections to multiple images in Adobe Bridge. The examples in this lesson do not go into depth in color correction, since those features are covered in Lesson 5, "Color Correcting like a Pro." You will be introduced to some simple corrections that you can make when production time is at a premium.

1 In Adobe Bridge, select the images of the beach; the file names should be **Hawaii_18.JPG** through **Hawaii_21.JPG**.

2 With all four images selected, right-click (Windows) or Ctrl+click (Mac OS), and select Open in Camera Raw from the context menu. The Camera Raw dialog box appears.

These are not true RAW images, but the Camera feature allows jpgs to be opened in the Camera raw plug-in as well. You will find out more about Camera Raw throughout multiple lessons in this book.

3 Click the Select All button in the upper-left area of the Camera Raw dialog box.

4 Next, click the White Balance tool (🖊) in the tools panel across the top, and click any of the grey clouds. Notice that all four of the images selected on the left side of the dialog box are corrected. The White Balance tool is not perfect, but it is a quick and easy tool that you can use to eliminate color casts in your image.

Balance all four images at once with the White Balance tool.

For the next part, you will visually improve the image using the Exposure and Contrast sliders. Keep in mind that this is an exercise in performing batch actions; you don't need to worry about exact settings and actual results at this time.

5 In the Basic section of the Camera Raw dialog box, click and drag the Exposure slider to the right to open up the exposure in this dark image just a bit.

6 Increase the contrast by dragging the Contrast slider to the right. Note that all four images are again corrected simultaneously.

7 Click Done and note that all four thumbnails are updated in Adobe Bridge.

You have completed the lesson on how to take advantage of Adobe Bridge.

Self study

Now that you have been exposed to some of the functionality in Adobe Bridge, try using it to organize all your files. Do the following:

1   Take a folder that you reference frequently and make it a favorite in Bridge.

2   Add keywords to a set of images using a metadata template that you create yourself.

3   Use batch rename on a folder of images that might have been imported with generic names from a digital camera, or rename the files in the advps02lessons folder again.

4   Select any three images and use the Load files as Photoshop Layers feature.

Review

Questions

1   Where do you find the Metadata template feature in Adobe Bridge?

2   Which workspace would be best to use if you wanted to see file information for your folder of images, such as Date Created, File Size, Type, Ratings, Keywords and more in a list view?

3   Name at least three search criteria that you can use to find files in Adobe Bridge.

Answers

1   You can find the Metadata template feature in the Tools menu.

2   To see your files in a list view with metadata details such as Date Created, File Size, Type, Ratings, Keywords, you would choose the metadata workspace.

3   You can find Photoshop image files in Adobe Bridge based upon any of these search criteria:

- Width
- Height
- Copyright notice
- Description
- Keywords
- Label
- Preserved Filename
- Rating
- Urgency
- EXIF information such as exposure, Focal length, ISO and more.

Lesson 3

What you'll learn in this lesson:

- Combining tools for the best selection
- Using Quick Selection
- Creating a mask
- Refining the edge
- About the Magic wand

Advanced Selection Techniques

The goal of making a great selection in Photoshop is to discreetly make selective changes. A beautiful composite, or retouched image, should not look contrived or unnatural…unless you are aiming for that look.

Starting up

You will work with several files from the advps03lessons folder in this lesson. Make sure that you have loaded the advpslessons folder onto your hard drive from the supplied DVD. For more detailed instructions, see "Loading lesson files" in the Starting up section of this book.

See Lesson 3 in action!

Use the accompanying video to gain a better understanding of how to use some of the features shown in this lesson. You can find the video tutorial for this lesson on the included DVD.

In this lesson, you will work with a folder of images to help you discover Adobe Bridge's advanced features.

1 In Adobe Photoshop choose File > Browse in Bridge to open Adobe Bridge.

2 Navigate to the advps03lessons folder, and open it so that the thumbnail images appear in the Content panel in Adobe Bridge.

3 Double-click to open the file named **advps0301.psd**. An image of a clock opens in Photoshop.

The clock image file.

4 Once the image is opened, choose File > Save As and type **advps0301_work** into the File name text field. Keep the Photoshop (PSD) format and make sure you are saving it in the advps03lessons folder. Click OK (Windows) or Save (Mac OS) when you are finished.

Review of the common selection tools

In this lesson, you'll cover the fundamentals that you must thoroughly understand before progressing into more advanced concepts. You will start off with a brief introduction to the selection tools. Since you are reading an advanced level book, the review will be concise because we assume that you are presently using many of these tools. Even as an advanced user, you should read this content over, since it covers additional tips and tricks that you might have missed in your experience with Photoshop.

Rectangular Marquee tool

The Rectangular Marquee tool (▭) tool allows you to create simple rectangular selections. Press **M** at any time to select the Rectangular Marquee tool.

Tips for using the Rectangular Marquee tool:

- If there are no other active selections in your image area, you can constrain the rectangular marquee selection to a square by pressing and holding the Shift key while clicking and dragging.

- You can begin a selection from the center by pressing and holding the Alt (Windows) or Option (Mac OS) key while dragging. Keep the selection constrained at the same time by pressing and holding the Alt/Option and the Shift key simultaneously while creating the selection.

Elliptical Marquee tool

The Elliptical Marquee tool (○) is the hidden tool for the Rectangular Marquee. You can get to it by pressing Shift+M, or by selecting the arrow in the lower-right corner of the Rectangular Marquee tool. Shift **M** toggles you back and forth between the Rectangular and Elliptical Marquee tools.

- If there are no other active selections in your image area, you can constrain the elliptical marquee selection to a circle by pressing and holding the Shift key while clicking and dragging.

- You can begin a selection from the center by pressing and holding the Alt (Windows) or Option (Mac OS) key while dragging. Keep the selection constrained at the same time by pressing and holding the Alt/Option and the Shift key simultaneously while creating the selection.

Building a selection

In this exercise, you have the opportunity of trying out some of the marquee tool tips. You will then take the selection a little further by saving and transforming the marquee selection.

1   With the **advps0301_work** image open, select the Elliptical Marquee tool.

2   Press and hold the Alt+Shift (Windows) or Option+Shift (Mac OS) keys, and then click the center of the clock face, where the base of the hands meet.

3   Click and drag outwards; notice that you selection starts from the center, rather than from one of the corners (which is the default). This can be very helpful when making selections of people (start with the nose) or objects such as wheels.

4   If the circle is not exactly up to the edge of the clock face, take your cursor (while you still have the Elliptical marquee selected) and click and drag to reposition it. The clock face is not perfectly circular, so do not worry if your marquee selection does not match up exactly.

*Click and drag from the center while holding the
Alt/Option+Shift keys.*

5   Choose File > Save. Keep the selection active and the file open.

Transforming your selection

A little known feature is the opportunity to scale, rotate, and even distort an existing selection. In this next part of the lesson, you scale the elliptical selection you just made. Right now you will change the selection so that it surrounds the entire clock.

1   With your selection still active, choose Select > Transform Selection; handles appear that you can use to adjust the selection.

2   Click the transform handles and drag in or out to better fit your selection to the clock face.

Use the handles to transform your selection.

3 Press the Enter (Windows) or Return (Mac OS) key when you are finished transforming the selection. You can also click the Commit (✓) button on the far right side of the control panel to confirm your transformation.

Saving your selection

Before going any further, it is a good idea to save the selection that you created. By saving a selection, you can easily return to the selection at a later time, or use it to add or delete from other selections.

1 Make sure that your selection is still active, and then choose Select > Save Selection.

2 In the Save Selection dialog box, type **clock face** into the Name text box, and then click OK, leaving the other settings as they are.

Save your selection for later use.

3 Keep the selection active for the next part of this lesson.

Transforming to create a second selection

You will now take the existing selection and use it to create a second selection.

1 Choose Select > Transform Selection; the Transform handles appear around your selection.

2 Press and hold the Alt (Windows) or Option (Mac OS) key, grab any of the corner selection handles, and drag outwards. By pressing and holding the Alt/Option key, you can force the scale to come from the center, rather than from the corner you drag.

3   Release when the selection reaches the outside of the clock. Note that the outside of the clock is not perfectly circular, so you will have to adjust the other handles to match the shape of the clock.

Press and hold the Alt/Option and drag a corner outwards.

4   Now click individual handles and click and drag to adjust the selection so that it better fits the outside of the clock. When you have adjusted the handles to match, press the Return/Enter key or click the Commit transform button located on the right side of the Options bar.

5   Choose Select > Save Selection, name this selection **clock outside**, and click OK.

6   Keep the selection active and the file open for the next part of the selection.

Combining your selections

Sometimes it is easier to combine selections to create a more difficult one. In this lesson, you take your two saved selections and use them to create the selection of the casing around the clock.

1   Make sure that you still have the outside of the clock selected. If you need to reselect the clock outside selection, choose Select > Load Selection and choose the channel named clock outside.

2   With the outside already selected, choose Select > Load Selection, and then choose the channel clock face. Do not click OK yet.

3 In the Operation section, choose Subtract from Selection, and then click OK.

Choose to subtract one selection from the other.   *The result.*

4 Save your new selection by choosing Select > Save Selection; name this selection **clock case**, and then click OK.

For additional practice, you will now experiment with curves in this selected area.

5 If you do not see the Layers panel, choose Windows > Layers now.

6 Select the Create new fill or adjustment layer button (●) at the bottom of the Layers panel, and select Curves; the Properties panel appears with the curve control on it.

7 Click the straight curve line to add at least five random anchor points, and then click and drag some of the anchor points up and others down in an alternating fashion. This should create a metallic look to the clock casing.

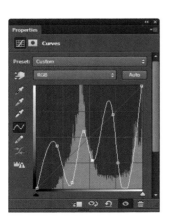

Add points to the curve and drag up or down.   *The result.*

8 You just created an adjustment layer, which can be turned off and on by checking the visibility (👁) icon to the right of the Curves 1 layer in the Layers panel. Notice that your selection was automatically turned into a mask that is applied only to that layer.

The new adjustment layer with mask.

As you can see, simple selections can be turned into more complex selections and masks if you know where to find those features. In the next section, we use some other basic selection tools, but also take you deeper into Photoshop selections that will help you to build more complex selections.

9 Choose File > Save and File > Close.

Taking the Lasso tool to the max

The Lasso tool (⌀) is one of the defaults methods for starting a selection. Unless you have a steady hand, you won't be able to count on achieving a precise selection with this tool, but it is a fine way to start if you choose to refine your selection, or plan on feathering (vignetting) to soften those imperfect selection edges.

Default Lasso tool

The Default Lasso tool (⌀) allows you to click and draw, just like a brush, to make a selection. When using this tool, you typically need to encompass the entire area that you want to select, starting and stopping at the same spot to create a closed selection.

Polygonal Lasso tool

Using the Polygonal Lasso tool (▧), you can click and release to create straight lines from one point to another. Use this tool to quickly make straight line selections. Using the Polygon Lasso tool is fast and easy; however, in Lesson 4, "The Pen Tool: Beyond the Primer", you will discover how to use the preferred method for making straight line selections, which is the Pen tool.

Magnetic Lasso tool

The Magnetic Lasso tool (⬚) allows you select a location on the edge of an object that you want to select. As you move your cursor along the object, the selection border snaps to the edges of the object in the image. Based on a few settings from you, Photoshop automatically adds points that create a selection when you close the selection process.

Alternating between the Polygonal and regular Lasso tool

You can easily switch between the Lasso tool and the Polygonal lasso tool, even if you are already in the middle of creating a selection. In this next section, you have an opportunity to mix a straight line polygon Lasso selection with a selection made with the more freeform Lasso tool.

1   Choose File > Browse in Bridge and open the file named **advps0302.psd** located in the advps03lessons folder. An image of popcorn appears.

2   Choose File > Save As, and in the File name text field, type **advps0302_work**. Make sure the file you are saving is in the Photoshop (PSD) format and that you are saving into the advps03lessons folder. Click Save.

3   If you cannot see the Polygonal Lasso tool (⬚), press and hold the Lasso tool to select it.

4   Click once on the top-right corner of the popcorn box, and then click the bottom–right side of the box. Notice that a segment is created, indicating the area that will be selected.

5   Continue to follow the edge of the box until you reach the top-left edge of the box.

Start by clicking in the   *Then click the lower-left*   *Continue until you reach the upper-left corner.*
upper-right corner of   *corner.*
the box.

If you want to undo the last click with the polygonal lasso tool, press the Delete key. If you want to abort the selection you have started, press the ESC key.

Now is when you will require a little bit more coordination. To select the popcorn, you will use a key modifier to switch the regular Lasso tool and click and drag to create that part of the selection.

6 Press and hold the Alt (Windows) or Option (Mac OS) key, and then click and drag around the top edge of the popcorn to make that selection. Do not worry if it is not perfect; as stated earlier, this lesson is all about using the techniques, and not about creating a perfect selection. Continue dragging (no clicking) until you get back to the point where you started the selection of the box, and then release.

Press and hold the Alt/Option key and drag to switch to the regular Lasso tool.

Pressing and holding the Alt/Option key toggles the Lasso tool regardless of the tool you start with, so you can go from the regular freeform Lasso tool to the Polygon Lasso tool as well.

7 From the Tools panels, select the Regular default Lasso tool ($\wp$).

8 Use the Zoom tool to zoom into the popcorn area of the image.

9 Refine your selection by pressing and holding the Shift key and encompassing any areas of popcorn that you missed. When pressing and holding the Shift key, you will see a plus sign next to the cursor ($\mathcal{P}$), indicating that you are adding to the selection.

10 Click and drag to completely surround an area in your image where you missed part of the popcorn selection. You must completely encompass this area and draw the selection from start to finish, not releasing the mouse until you reach the original start point.

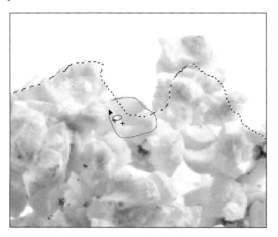

Shift+click and drag to encompass the missed popcorn.

11 If you went too far in a selection and want to remove some of the areas you selected, press and hold the Alt (Windows) or Option (Mac OS) key and encompass the area that you want to deselect. When pressing and holding the Alt/Option key, the minus sign appears next to the cursor (minus selection).

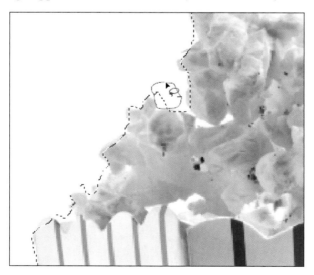

Alt/Option+Click and drag to deselect an area.

12 Turn your selection into a layer mask by clicking the Add layer mask button at the bottom of the Layers panel. The popcorn box is now on a transparent layer. You will find out more about tasks you can carry out with layer masks throughout the following lessons in this book.

13 Choose File > Save and keep this file open for the next part of the lesson.

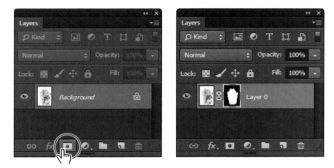

Turn your selection into a layer mask.   *The result.*

Adding and deleting using the tool Options

Using the Shift+Alt/Option key to add and subtract from a selection is a quick and easy way to keep you productive. If you would prefer not to use shortcuts, you can use the Selection options that are available in the Options bar of the selection tools. In the Options bar, you see four buttons, each representing the selection mode.

A. *New selection.* **B.** *Add to selection.*
C. *Subtract from selection.* **D.** *Intersect with selection.*

As a default, the Lasso tool is set to create a new selection every time you release and begin creating a new selection. You essentially override that selection by pressing and holding the Shift+key when adding to a selection. If you would rather not use a key modifier, you can make these choices in the Options bar, and not have to use the Shift key or Alt/Option key. The benefit to using the key modifiers is that you do not get unexpected results if you accidently leave the default at a different selection in the Options bar.

Covering up a non-perfect selection

In the previous exercise, you created a rather quick selection, and then went back to improve it by adding and deleting to the selected area. There are many methods that you can use to create selections; the Lasso tool is not the most precise, but it still works in an emergency and is suitable if you want to feather or apply a vignette to the edges of your selections. Using the Properties panel you can interactively feather, or soften, the edges of your layer mask.

1 If you do not see the Properties panel, choose Windows > Properties. The Properties panel is a dynamic panel that changes depending upon your selection. Since you still have your layer mask selected, the Layers panel shows the properties of your mask. In this lesson, you will feather the selection to soften the edges.

2 Click and drag the slider control in the Feather slider over to the right until it reaches the 5 mark, or type **5** in the Feather text box. Notice how the edges of your selection are softened.

Soften the edges by feathering the mask. *The result.*

A great feature of the Properties panel is that it lets you easily remove the feathering on the layer mask by sliding the slider back to 0 (zero).

3 Experiment adding more and less feathering to your mask by using the Feather slider. When you are finished experimenting, return to the 5 value.

4 Choose File > Save, and then File > Close.

About the Quick Selection tool

The Quick Selection tool was introduced several versions ago and is probably one of the best ways to start a selection. By using the Quick Selection tool as a brush, you can make selections of areas that are similar in color. In this next section, you will make a selection using the Quick Selection tool, and then refine it using Refine Edge. The Refine Edge feature is powerful, and you will explore this feature more throughout this book; for now, you will use this feature in its simplest form.

1   Choose File > Browse in Bridge and open the file named **advps0303.psd**. A portrait of a woman appears.

2   Choose File > Save As. In the Save As dialog box, type **advps0303_work.psd** in the File Name text field. Make sure it is in the Photoshop (PSD) format and that you are saving the file into the advps03lessons folder. Click Save.

3   Select the Quick Selection tool (🖌) and start painting the woman; notice that you are painting the selection. You do not have controls to change the range of colors that are being selected, but you can change the width of the brush to select smaller or larger areas.

4   Press the Right Bracket (]) key; notice that the brush size for the Quick Selection tool becomes larger. Press the Left Bracket ([) key; notice that the brush size becomes smaller.

Don't worry about getting a great selection of the hair on the woman; do the best you can to get up to the edge of her hair without selecting a large span of the background.

Paint the woman using the Quick Selection tool to make a selection.

5   If you paint too far and select too much, press and hold the Alt key (Windows) or Option key (Mac OS) and paint over that region again.

6   Choose File > Save; keep your selection active for the next part of the lesson.

Refining your selection

In this next section, you use the Refine Edge feature to improve your selection.

1   With the selection of the woman still active, click the Refine Edge button in the Options bar. The Refine Edge dialog box appears. The Refine Edge feature is available in the options of all the selection tools.

2   Press **F** to cycle through the different view modes that are available for you to work in while in the Refine Edge dialog box. The backgrounds that you see, appearing behind your selection, are not permanent and are meant to help you better see your selection refinements.

If you want more details about each view mode, click and hold the arrow to the right of the View preview. Hover over each View mode until a tool tip appears. Show Original displays the original selection for comparison. Show Radius displays the selection border where edge refinement occurs.

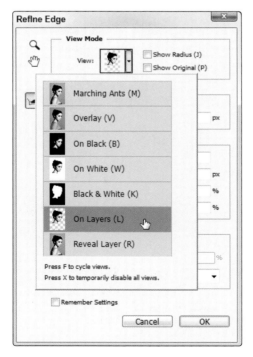

Choose a view mode that will make it easier for you to see your selection refinements.

3 For this exercise, click the View drop-down menu and choose On Layers. This makes the background transparent. If you had additional layers underneath this image, they would appear now.

4 Select the Refine Radius tool (▣).The Refine Radius tool allows you to precisely adjust the border area in which edge refinement occurs. You will use it around her hair.

5 Notice that as you paint, the border of your selection is being refined to include the wisps of hair. The background that is showing through the wisps of hair is also erased. Continue painting until you have selected the fine pieces of hair. You can control the radius of the Refine Radius tool by pressing the Left ([) and Right (]) Bracket keys.

Select the Refine Radius tool.   *Paint around the hair area.*

6 If you cannot see the details in the hair area, use the Zoom tool located in the upper-left area of the Refine Edge dialog box to zoom in to the section that you just refined.

It is possible to over-refine an area by brushing too far into the image area that you want to select. If that occurs, erase your refinements.

7 Press Shift+E; notice that your cursor now has a − (minus sign) in it instead of a + (plus sign). You just switched to the Erase refinement tool. Alternatively, you can also use the Erase refinement tool (▣) by clicking and holding the Refine Radius tool. Experiment by brushing with the Erase Refinements tool. Press Shift+E to return to the Refine Radius tool if you need to retouch the area again.

8 Once you have a selection, choose Layer Mask from the Output To drop-down menu in the Output section of the Refine Edge dialog box.

9 Click OK; notice that the Background layer is now Layer 0 and has a layer mask.

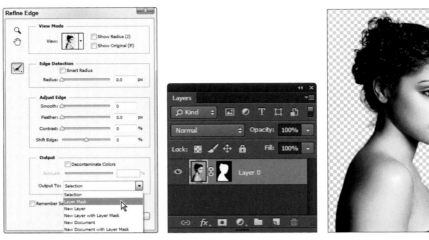

Choose Layer Mask from the Out To menu.

A layer mask has been added based upon your selection.

The result.

10 Choose File > Save, and then choose File > Close.

When to use Edge Detection

In the Refine Edge dialog box, you have an option of turning on Edge Detection. Edge Detection works on the entire image, and can be helpful when you select something furry or an overall texture on all sides. However, this tool is not appropriate for images that have varying amounts of texture and smoothness on the edges.

Edge detection allows you to set an amount, or radius, that determines the distance around the edge of your selection that you would like to refine. For a dog with long fur, this would be a larger amount. For a tennis ball, this might be a smaller amount.

Smart Radius automatically adjusts the radius for hard and soft edges found in the border region. Deselect this option if the border is uniformly hard or soft-edged, or if you want to control the Radius setting and refinement brushes more precisely.

A furry dog requires a larger radius.   *The result.*

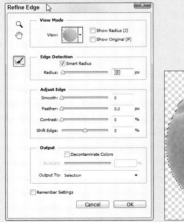

A smoother surface, such as this tennis ball, requires a smaller radius.   *The result.*

Going beyond the Magic Wand

The Magic Wand is the old standby tool for making quick selections. You typically can't use it to create an excellent selection on its own, but it is a great tool for starting your selection.

The Magic Wand tool makes a selection based upon the similarities of tone and color, but it can go beyond that with a few adjustments.

1 Choose File > Browse in Bridge, or File > Open and navigate to the advps03lessons folder. Locate the image named **advps0304.psd** and open it in Photoshop; an image of very bright flowers appears.

2 Choose File > Save As, and in the File name text field, type **advps0304_work**. Make sure that you are saving in the Photoshop (PSD) format and into the advps03lessons folder. Click Save.

3 Select the Magic Wand tool (✳) and click the green flower in the image. Depending upon the shade of green you click, a range of the green colors is activated in the image. If you are at the default tolerance of 32, you should expect to have selected only a small range of the green color. To check your tolerance, locate the Tolerance text box in the Options bar when you have the Magic Wand selected. If necessary, change the value to 32 now.

4 Now press and hold the Shift key and click any green areas that were missed. By pressing and holding the Shift key, you can add to the selection.

Add to your selection by Shift+clicking with the Magic Wand tool.

5   Press Ctrl+D (Windows) or Command+D (Mac OS) to deselect your selection.

6   Look back in the Options bar at the top; notice that the Magic Wand's tolerance is set to select 32 shades or levels of color. This is 32 out of 255, so a rather small selection is being made as a default.

7   Position your cursor over the word Tolerance (in the Options bar) and drag; notice that you can adjust the value as though you were using a slider. You can use this method to increase and decrease values in the Options bar. In our example, the value was changed to 100. Slide across until you reach the approximate value of 100, or type **100** into the Tolerance text field.

8   Using the Magic Wand, click again on the green flower; more of the green is selected.

Increase the Tolerance to 100.

The increase in tolerance increases the selection.

9   Now deselect by pressing Ctrl+D (Windows) or Command+D (Mac OS).

10 In the Options bar, uncheck Contiguous. By unchecking Contiguous, which means touching, you can select all the green color within your tolerance range in the image with one click.

11 Click again on the green flower to see that now the selection goes beyond the initial selection, activating areas with a similar range of the green color throughout the image.

Uncheck Contiguous.

The selection now extends beyond the touching colors.

12 Instead of Shift+clicking, choose Select > Grow. The Grow feature looks at the present Tolerance setting and increases your selection based upon that value. You might notice that the 100 setting in the Tolerance took the expanded selection too far. In this next step, you will see how you can change this value every time you choose to Grow.

13 Press Ctrl+Z (Windows) or Command+Z (Mac OS) to undo your last step.

14 Enter the value of **50** into the Tolerance text box in the Options bar.

15 Choose Select > Grow to see a much less drastic expansion of your selection.

Cleaning up your selection with Quick Mask

You now have an opportunity to practice your selection skills by using Quick Mask to quickly add the hard-to-select sections that are dramatically out of the tolerance range.

1   Press **Q** to enter into the Quick Mask mode. The Quick Mask mode shows the selected area in your image as clear, and your unselected (masked area) as a reddish orange color. If you are from the printing or pre-press industry, you would recognize the similarity of this color to a traditional masking product called amberlith or rubylith.

Quick Mask mode shows the masked area as orange.

2   Select the Brush tool and press **D**, which defaults your foreground and background back to the default black and white setting.

3   For the next part, you want to make sure that White is the foreground color. If it is not, press **X**, which is the keyboard shortcut to swap your foreground and background colors.

4   Select your Brush tool and position it over one of the areas in the flower that were masked, but are not supposed to be. In the next step, you will paint these parts of the mask out with white, which is clear in the Quick Mask mode.

5   If your brush size is too large to easily paint over the masked areas in the green flower, press Ctrl+[(Left bracket) (Windows) or Command+[(Left bracket) (Mac OS) as many times as necessary.

If necessary, make your brush size small enough to paint the masked areas in the green flower.

6   Carefully paint with the Brush tool over the masked areas in the green flower that you want to select. If you accidently go too far, press Ctrl+Z (Windows) or Command+Z (Mac OS), or press **X** to swap back to black to re-paint your mask. Continue working until there is no mask material on the green flower.

Paint over the masked area on the green flower to remove the mask.

7 Press **Q** to toggle back to the Standard mode where you can see your selection. If you need to edit more, press **Q** again to continue editing the mask with the Brush tool.

8 When you are finished, make sure you are back in the Standard mode by pressing Q, and then choose Select > Save Selection. Name your selection **Green Flower** and click OK.

9 Choose File > Save to save your work file, and then choose File > Close.

Self study

Now that you have more experience with some of the selection tools, you can experiment on your own with some additional images. Open the image named **advps03_Magic_Wand.psd** located in the advps03lessons and follow these steps:

1   Set your Magic Wand tool to the correct settings to select the shovel and the other two yellow toys in this image.

2   Enter the Quick Mask mode to clean up the selections.

3   Save your selection.

You can also practice your refine selection skills by opening **advps03_Refine_Selection.psd** from the advps03lessons folder. Using the Refine Edge feature you used in this lesson, refine the selection of this model's hair.

Review

Questions

1   What are the consistent keyboard modifiers for adding and deleting to a selection?

2   How can you dynamically feather a mask in a manner that can easily be edited at a later time?

3   When using the Magic Wand tool, what option can you turn off to select a range of colors throughout an image whether it is touching or not?

Answers

1   The consistent key modifiers for adding and deleting selections are the Shift key for adding to an existing selection, and the Alt/Option key for deleting from a selection.

2   To change the feather of a mask, you should feather the mask by using the Window > Properties panel. Make sure that you have your layer mask selected, and then use the slider in the Properties panel to feather your selection.

3   If you want to select a range of colors throughout your image file using the Magic Wand tool, you can turn off the Contiguous check box located in the Options bar.

What you'll learn in this lesson:

- Creating curve and anchor points
- Creating a vector mask
- Using a path for filter effects
- Applying a custom brush to a path
- Saving your transparent image

The Pen Tool: Beyond the Primer

Many users do not realize the potential of the vector tools and features available in Photoshop. If you can save the time of integrating your image with Illustrator or InDesign, why not complete your vector objects directly in Photoshop?

Starting up

You will work with several files from the advps04lessons folder in this lesson. Make sure that you have loaded the advpslessons folder onto your hard drive from the supplied DVD. For more detailed instructions, see "Loading lesson files" in the Starting up section of this book.

See Lesson 4 in action!

Use the accompanying video to gain a better understanding of how to use some of the features shown in this lesson. You can find the video tutorial for this lesson on the included DVD.

In this lesson, you will review some of the fundamental Pen tool features and functions. This lesson will be a great review for those who already use the Pen tool and will probably teach you some new tricks. Those who have not been formally instructed on how to use the Pen tool should feel confident enough to recreate any shape with the Pen tool after completing this lesson. Be patient if you think this lesson might be starting out slow; it is important to build your Pen tool skills to a level where you can create more complex paths throughout the remainder of this book.

Practicing with the Pen tool

In this first section, you will create a new document and practice basic Pen features.

1   Choose File > New and choose Default Photoshop size from the Preset drop-down menu. Click OK to accept the defaults. A blank image area appears.

2   Select the Pen tool. Look at the Options bar, and then confirm that your Pen tool is set up to create a Path by clicking the Pick a tool mode drop-down menu and verifying it is set to Path.

Make sure that you are in the Path mode.

3   Select the Pen tool and position it anywhere over the image area; notice that the Pen tool cursor shows you an asterisk (*), indicating that you are creating a new path.

4   Press your Caps Lock key on the keyboard; notice that your Pen tool cursor is now set as Precision cursor. You should note that the Caps Lock key is a toggle key that will turn this view of your cursor off and on.

5   Turn off Caps Lock.

6   With the regular cursor (Caps lock released), click to create an anchor point. Notice that the anchor point is created at the very tip of the Pen tool.

7   Press Cap Locks again and then click. When using the Precision cursor, you create an anchor point in the intersection of the cursor.

8   Turn off Caps Lock.

The regular cursor creates an anchor point at the tip.   *The Precision cursor creates an anchor point in the intersection.*

9   Press Ctrl+A (Windows) or Command+A (Mac OS), and then press the Delete or Backspace key to delete any paths that have been started on this document. Keep this blank file open for the next part of the lesson.

Creating controlled paths

In this next section, you will take the Pen tool further by discovering how to precisely control the paths that you create. You will start out by gaining a basic understanding of how you can modify your paths as you work.

1   Make sure that your Pen tool is active, and then click once anywhere in the image area.

2   Click anywhere else; note that one anchor point connects to another. Unlike Illustrator, you do not see a stroke when you create paths in Photoshop. This is because paths in Photoshop are generally not used to create shapes, even though they can be, but are mostly used to create precise selections and masks.

3   Shift+click to another location; notice that by pressing and holding the Shift key, you can constrain the path to be on a 45°, 90°, or 180° angle.

4   Now, click and drag to create directional lines. As you adjust the lines, the angle and size of your curved path is changed. Controlling these directional paths can be complicated until you understand how to work with them. This is the focus of the next section in this lesson.

5   Choose File > Close, and choose not to save the changes to this file.

About precision creation of Pen paths

In this part of the lesson, you will open a file that you will use as a template to practice controlling directional lines and curved paths. You will start by opening the template and setting up guides.

1   Choose File > Browse in Bridge; locate the file named **advps0401_start.psd** and open it in Photoshop CC.

2   Notice that the Photoshop file includes a Background layer and an active layer for you to practice your own Pen path.

Creating guides

You will start by creating guides that will help you make sure you are creating anchor points in the right place.

1   Press Ctrl+R (Windows) or Command+R (Mac OS) to make sure that you can see the Rulers.

2 Click the Horizontal ruler at the top and drag a guide from the ruler down to the baseline of the arches in the topmost shape.

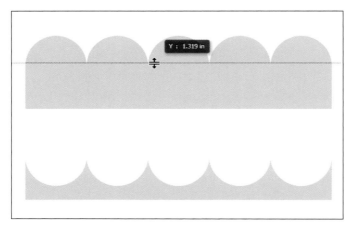

Click and drag guides to help you create precise Pen paths.

3 Click and drag another guide and position it at the top of the arches.

4 Choose File > Save; in the Save As dialog box field, type **advps0401_work** into the File name text field. Make sure that you are saving the file in the advps04lessons folder and keep the format as Photoshop. Click Save.

Beginning the Pen path

You will now start your Pen path.

1 Start by clicking the lower-right corner of the top shape, and then Shift+clicking the lower-left corner.

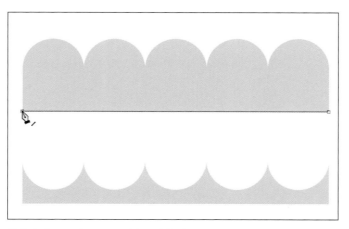

Click the lower-right corner and then Shift+click the lower-left corner.

2 Select the Zoom tool (🔍), and if checked, uncheck Scrubby Zoom in the Options bar. Without Scrubby Zoom selected, you have the ability to click and drag to create a marquee selection of an area that you want to zoom into.

3 Press and hold the Ctrl+Spacebar (Windows) or Command+Spacebar (Mac OS); click and drag the left side of the topmost shape to zoom into the area where the first arch appears in this shape.

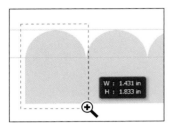

Click and drag to zoom into the first arch.

4 Shift+click the last part of the straight area on the left, right before the shape starts to turn into an arch. This is also the location of the first guide that you created.

Shift-click again to create the small straight segment on the left side.

5 Now click and drag upwards to create a directional line before you create the path that creates the arch. By clicking and dragging the directional line first, you can create a much wider curved path.

When you create arches, you must drag the directional line in the direction of the arch, which is up in this case. Also, you must not pull the directional line past the arch that you are about to create.

Click and drag straight up until the directional line is slightly higher than the top of the arch. You should drag slightly higher than the second guide that you created.

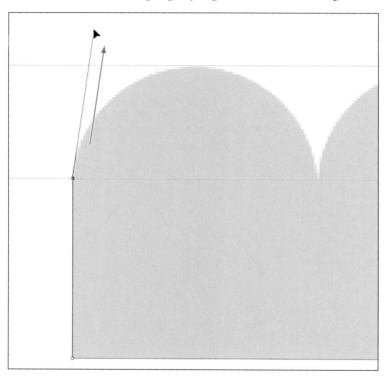

Click and drag before creating the arch.

Press and hold the Shift key to constrain a directional line and help keep it straight.

6 Click and drag down the base on the other side of the arch; keep dragging the directional line and repositioning until the path that you are creating closely matches the arch. If you cannot align it perfectly, it could have to do with your original directional line. You will learn to edit this in the next set of steps.

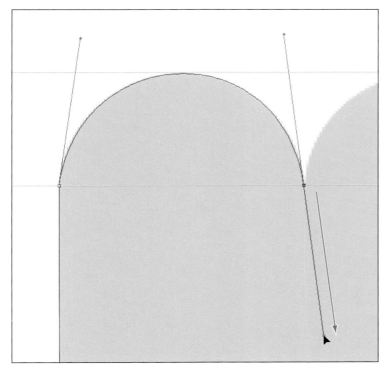

Click and drag to finish the arch.

7 Press Ctrl+S (Windows) or Command+S (Mac OS) to save this file.

Editing your arch

In this next set of steps, you will use the Direct Selection tool to edit your path.

1 Click and hold the Selection tool (▶) to select the hidden Direct Selection tool (▷).

2 With the Direct Selection tool, reposition the directional lines or anchor points if necessary.

3 Select the Pen tool again, and choose File > Save if you made any changes with the Direct Selection tool.

Continuing the path

You will now continue the path. Note that new methods for creating these paths will be introduced along the way.

The last point is a curved anchor point, meaning that if you were to click and drag another path from that anchor point, it would create a curve. This is because you clicked and dragged when you created the originating anchor point. This can sometimes be frustrating, especially when you need to create a sharp corner such as between the arches in this template. Fortunately, you can convert this curved anchor point into a corner anchor point with a simple key modifier, the Alt (Windows) or Option (Mac OS) key.

1   With the Pen tool selected, position your cursor over the last anchor point that you created. You see the Pen cursor and then a diagonal line segment (╲). The presence of this line segment indicates that you are hovering directly over the anchor point, but do not click at this time.

2   Press and hold the Alt (Windows) or Option (Mac OS) key and look for the line to turn into a carat (∧).

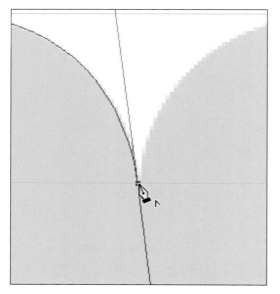

Position the Pen tool cursor over the last anchor point and press and hold the Alt/Option key.

3   Click and drag up to create the directional line for the next arch. Follow the same method that you used for the original arch, making the directional line slightly higher than the arch.

4   Now click the other side of the arch and click and drag down, forming the arched path as you drag.

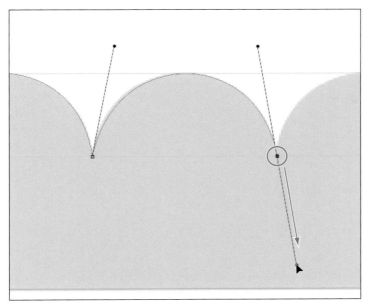

Click and drag the other side of the arch to form the path.

If necessary, press and hold the Spacebar to temporarily turn your cursor into the hand tool, and then click and drag the exercise image over into view.

5   Press and hold the Alt/Option key again; click and drag up to form the directional line for the next arch, and then click and drag down the other side of the arch.

In the next step, you will try a variation of the method you have been using; this time you will not release the mouse before pressing and holding the alt/option key.

6   Press and hold the Alt/Option key and drag up to make your directional line for the next arch.

7   Click and drag the other side of the arch to form the arched path, but do not release the mouse.

8   Before you release, press and hold the Alt/Option key. This creates the corner anchor point on the fly; you can now drag upwards to create the next arch. Using this method helps keep the task of creating a path quick and efficient.

9   If you are not at the end of the arches, continue creating your path until you are at the end and then Alt/Option+click your last point. It might not look like a curve point; this is because you created the last anchor point while dragging down.

10 Press and hold the Shift key and click your starting anchor point. A circle appears to the right of your cursor when you hover over the anchor point.

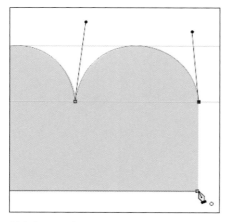

Click the original anchor point when you see a circle appear to the right of your cursor.

Now you will move on to the next exercise. You will not be taken through every step as you were in the initial exercise; much of the techniques you will use in the next exercise are similar to what you have just learned.

1 Press Ctrl+0 (Windows) or Command+0 (Mac OS) to fit the image into your work area.

2 Click and drag a guide the horizontal ruler at the top and drag it down to the tips of the lower Exercise 2 shape.

3 Using the Pen tool, click the lower-right corner and then Shift+click the lower-left corner.

4 Click the upper-left corner. Zoom in to the first downward arch.

5 Click and drag downwards to create the directional line for the arch that is going down.

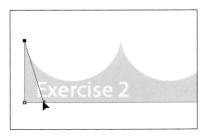

Click and drag down to create the directional line for the downward arch.

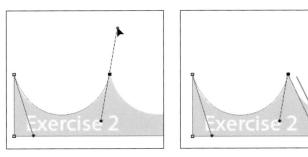

Click and drag up.

Before releasing, press and hold the Alt/Option key and swing the directional line down.

6 Click and drag the other side of the arch to form the second arched path.

7 Now finish this shape on your own.

8 You can choose File > Save, and then File > Close to close this file.

Practicing with an image

Now that you have had an opportunity to practice your Pen tool fundamentals, you will apply what you have learned to create a mask on an image.

In this next part of the lesson, you will use the Pen tool to select an object that might be difficult to select with the standard selection tools. You will then incorporate text and a vector shape to see how you can take advantage of the vector tools in Photoshop.

1 Choose File > Open and navigate to the advps04lessons folder. Open the file named **advps0402_start.psd**; an image of a gumball machine appears.

2 Choose File > Save. In the Save As dialog box, type **advps0402_work** into the File name text field. Navigate to the advps04lessons folder and make sure it is in the Photoshop format. Click Save.

3   Select the Zoom tool and make sure that Scrubby Zoom is turned off in the Options panel. You will use keyboard shortcuts to zoom in and out and to navigate this image as you create the Pen path.

To create a successful Pen path, you need to be zoomed in the image. Start in the upper-left side of the glass bowl.

4   With the Zoom tool selected, click and drag to zoom into the top glass area of the gumball machine.

Click and drag to zoom in to the   *The zoom result.*
gumball machine.

> *As you zoom in, you might see the pixel grid feature. If the grid is distracting, choose View Show > Pixel Grid to turn off the pixels grid.*

You will be instructed on how to start the Pen path around the gumball machine, but will not be taken through every path segment. As you follow the steps, you should start feeling more comfortable with the Pen tool and how to control the path using the directional lines, as well as with some of the shortcuts used for altering your path.

5   Start at the top-left part of the glass and click and drag to create a directional line that reaches the approximate width of the glass jar. As you start gaining skills with the Pen tool, you start to recognize arcs in the shapes of objects.

6   Position your cursor further in the curve of the glass and click and drag; adjust the directional lines until the path segment follows the curve of the glass.

Click and drag to create the first directional line.   *Continue with another click and drag further down the glass.*

7   Press and hold the Ctrl+Spacebar (Windows) or Command+Spacebar (Mac OS) and drag to zoom into the bottom of the glass area.

Use keyboard shortcuts for zooming.

8 The next curve that you are creating is much shallower. If you were to click the next point and drag, you would have a large looping curve. To avoid this, press and hold the Alt (Windows) or Option (Mac OS) key and click and drag the second half of the last directional line up towards the associated anchor point. Make sure that you keep the directional line on the same angle; you are converting that anchor point from a smooth one to a corner point. It won't be noticeable unless you change the angle of the second half of the directional line.

9 Click down towards the bottom of the glass bowl to continue the path.

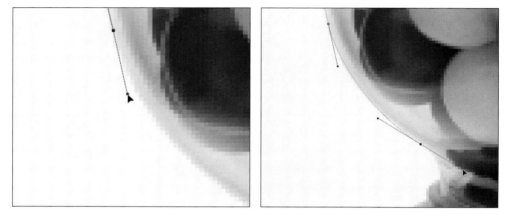

Press and hold the Alt/Option key.

Drag the bottom directional line back towards the anchor point.

10 Again, you are entering an area with a much smaller curve, so press and hold the Alt/Option key down to shorten the second half of the directional line. Once you have reduced the length of the second half of the directional line, click and drag to create your next arch. For the placement of this anchor point, look for the tiny rim of the glass top.

11 Press Alt/Option+click the last anchor point to turn it into a corner point so you can capture the small rim.

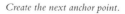

Shorten the directional path.

Create the next anchor point.

Press and hold the Alt/Option key and drag the directional line to shorten it.

12 Click into capture the rim, and then click down to create a corner anchor point right at the edge of the next curve. Next, you will generate a curved path that will be generated from the last corner anchor point you created.

13 Press and hold the Alt/Option key and drag a directional line out of the last anchor point that you created. Follow the next curve that you are creating, and then click the other side of the curve to create your arch but do not release, instead press and hold the Alt/Option key and immediately and drag your directional path out for the next curve. You are now in the red base area of the gumball machine.

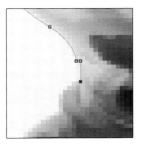
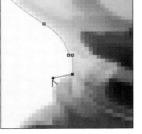
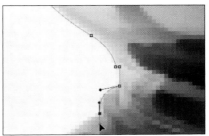

Click to create the corner anchor points for the rim.

Alt/Option+click to pull a directional line from the corner point.

Click and drag to continue the curve.

If you need to scroll while using the Pen tool, press and hold the Spacebar; your cursor turns into the Hand tool and you can quickly click and drag to reposition your visible area of the image.

14 Click the other side of the curve at the top of the gumball machine. Note that your next path is straight, which means that you need to press and hold your Alt/Option key on that last anchor point to turn it into a corner point.

15 Press and hold the Alt/Option key and hover over the anchor point until you see the cursor appear with a carat, and then click. The second half of the direction line appears and you can scroll down to the base of the gum machine and click.

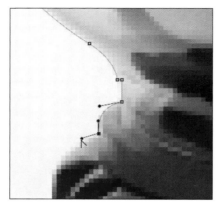 

Alt/Option click.   *Click at the base of the gum machine.*

16 At this point in the lesson, you have covered all the different Pen path variations that you need to know to complete the path around the rest of the gumball machine. Do your best to follow the gumball machine on your own, but follow these important tips:

- Zoom in and out frequently to make sure you are following the image. Remember to press Ctrl+Spacebar (Windows) or Command+Spacebar (Mac OS) to zoom in. To zoom back out, it is easier to press Ctrl/Command+0 (zero) and then reset the zoom level as needed.

- Press and hold the Ctrl/Command key to access the Direct Selection tool when you want to edit the placement of an anchor point or the length and direction of a directional line. When you release the Ctrl/Command key, your Pen tool is still selected and you can continue your path.

- If you make a mistake, press Ctrl+Z (Windows) or Command+Z (Mac OS), since it will keep you path active.

- If you need to move an anchor point right after you click to create it, press and hold the Spacebar to reposition it. When you release, your Pen tool is still active.

- To change direction or go from a curve to a straight path, press and hold the Alt/Option key and click the last anchor point when you see the carat symbol next to the cursor (▶).

- To create a curve from a straight anchor point, click and drag a directional line from the anchor point. Follow the direction and angle of the curve.

- When ending the pen path, Alt/Option+click the last point to close the shape. You need to do this because you clicked and dragged the initial point, making it a curved anchor point.

Saving your path

In this next part of the exercise, you will save your completed path for use as a selection and mask. Now that you have a closed path, you will save it for later use.

1   With the file **adps0402_work.psd** still open, choose Window > Paths to see the Paths panel. In the Paths panel, you see a Work Path. You see a saved path already here that you will use later in this Lesson.

2   Press and hold the Alt/Option key and drag the Work Path down to the Create new path icon at the bottom of the Paths window. By pressing and holding the Alt/Option key, you will have the option of naming the path as it is being saved.

3   When the Save Path dialog box appears, type **gumball machine** into the Name text field. Click OK.

4   The Work Path remains, but will disappear from the Paths panel when that path is no longer active.

Save your path.

5   Choose File > Save to save the **advps0402_work** file.

What you can do with a path

You can take advantage of many opportunities once you have created a path. With a path you can:

• Load your path as a selection

• Use the path as a vector mask

• Stroke a path with the Brush tool

• Use multiple paths to create complex selections

• Export an image with transparency for use in applications that do not support native Photoshop images.

Loading your path as a selection

Pen paths and selections are very similar, since both can be used as selections, but there might be times when you would need a pixel selection to integrate with existing selections or use with certain tools, just as occurs with other selection tools.

1   With your **advps0402_work.psd** file open, go to the Paths panel.

2 Press and hold the Ctrl (Windows) or Command (Mac OS) key, and then click the gumball machine Path thumbnail in the Paths panel. This creates a pixel selection of your path. You path still exists, but it has been deactivated.

In the Paths panel, there is another path that has already been created for you; the second path is named Front Panel. By using the same modifier keys that you use for selections, you can add or delete other paths to a selection.

3 Press and hold the Ctrl+Alt (Windows) or Command+Option (Mac OS) key and hover over the thumbnail for the front panel path; a dashed line with a minus sign appears. Click and notice that the front panel path has been subtracted from the gumball machine selection. You will now use this selection to lighten the gumball machine.

Press and hold Ctrl+Shift (Windows) or Command+Shift (Mac OS) to add a path to a selection.

You can add or deselect from selection using paths.   *The resulting selection.*

4 If your Layers panel is not visible, choose Window > Layers now.

5 With your selection still active, select the Create new fill or adjustment layer button and choose Curves; the Properties panel appears with the Curves control. You will create a simple curve adjustment that will lighten the midtones.

6   Click the center of the Curves path and drag up. This adds an anchor point to the curve and adjusts your tonal value in the midtones of your image. By dragging up, you are lightening the image. Don't go too far, since you can degrade your image and lose some of the nice subtle values in it. Make a slight change and then close the Properties panel.

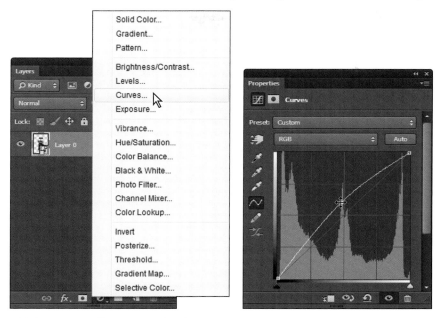

Click the Create new fill or adjustment layer button and select curves.   *Make a small midtone adjustment.*

7   Notice that you have created a mask in your Layers panel. The mask controls where the curves adjustment that you just made takes place. You will work on the front plate section later in this lesson.

You created a mask from your selection.

8   Choose File > Save. Keep the file open for the next part of this lesson.

Creating a vector mask of the gumball machine

When creating a silhouette, you should have a very clean and precise selection. This is when the Pen tool comes in handy.

1   With the **advps0402_work** file still open, select the gumball machine path in the Paths panel.

2   Locate your Layers panel and then select the bottom layer.

3   Press and hold the Ctrl (Windows) or Command (Mac OS) key and click the Add layer mask button at the bottom. By pressing and holding the Command key, you create a vector mask.

Create a vector mask from your active path.

4   Select the Direct Selection tool and activate the path. Note that the anchor points still exist and that you can edit the vector mask. If you make any changes, make sure to press Ctrl/Command+Z.

5   Choose File > Save. Keep this file open for the next part of the lesson.

Using a Pen path to create a Smart filter selection

As mentioned earlier in the lesson, sometimes the best way to make a selection is with the Pen tool. For instance, when you consider the best way to make a selection of just the front panel, it makes sense to use a tool that offers the ability to make straight line selections. Although the Polygonal tool (🖐) hidden in the regular Lasso tool offers this option, it does not offer the ability to tweak, or easily edit the selection.

Before starting, you will turn your Background layer into a Smart Object.

1   Right-click (Windows) or Ctrl+click (Mac OS) Layer 0 in the Layers panel and select Convert to Smart Object. By converting this layer to a Smart Object, you are embedding the layer image information into the Photoshop file. This is helpful when you want to make changes, such as resizing or applying filters, but still have the original digital content to refer back to.

2   Now press and hold the Ctrl key (Windows) or the Command key (Mac OS) and click the front panel path thumbnail in the Paths panel. This turns the path into an active selection. You will now apply the Unsharp mask filter.

Applying Unsharp mask to the selection

Unsharp masking is a traditional film compositing technique used to sharpen edges in an image. The Unsharp Mask filter corrects blurring in the image, and it compensates for blurring that occurs during the resampling and printing process. We highly recommend applying the Unsharp Mask filter whether your final destination is in print or online.

The Unsharp Mask filter assesses the brightness levels of adjacent pixels and increases their relative contrast: it lightens the light pixels that are located next to darker pixels as it darkens those darker pixels. You set the extent and range of lightening and darkening that occurs using the sliders in the Unsharp Mask dialog box. When sharpening an image, you should understand that the effects of the Unsharp Mask filter are far more pronounced on the screen than in high-resolution output, such as a printed piece.

1   Choose Filter > Sharpen > Unsharp Mask. Unsharp mask is an interesting term, because it is actually a technique used to sharpen the details in an image.

The Unsharp Mask dialog box appears.

2   In the Amount text field, enter **200**. The Amount value determines how much the contrast of pixels is increased. Typically, an amount of 150 percent or more is applied, but this amount is reliant on the subject matter. Overdoing Unsharp Mask on a person's face can be rather harsh, so that value can be set lower (150 percent) compared to an image of a piece of equipment, where fine detail is important (300 percent+).

3   Click and hold the preview to turn off the Unsharp mask filter preview. Release to see the Unsharp Mask filter applied.

4   Leave the Radius set to 1.0. This radius determines the number of pixels surrounding the edge pixels that are affected by the sharpening. For high-resolution images, a radius between 1 and 2 is recommended. If you are creating oversized posters and billboards, you might try experimenting with larger values.

5 Type **10** in the Threshold text field. The Threshold determines how different the brightness values between two pixels must be before they are considered edge pixels and are thus sharpened by the filter. To avoid introducing unwanted noise into your image, a minimum Threshold setting of 10 is recommended.

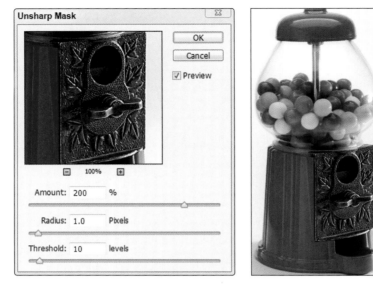

Choose to sharpen only the selected front panel.   The result is a sharp front panel.

6 Click OK; look at your Layers panel and notice that the filter was added as well as a Filter effects mask thumbnail.

7 Turn off and back on the Unsharp mask effect by clicking the visibility icon (👁) to the left of the Unsharp Mask effect in the Layers panel. You can easily remove a filter effect when it is applied to a Smart Object.

You will keep this filter effect in this exercise, but if you need to completely remove a filter, you can drag it to the Trash can icon in the lower portion of your Layers panel.

8 Double-click Unsharp Mask in the Layers panel; notice that the filter effect is editable. This action does not apply a second Unsharp mask filter to your image, but lets you edit the existing Filter effect.

9 Change the value in the Amount text field to **225**, and then click OK.

The mask was automatically created by your selection when you selected to apply the Unsharp mask filter, but you can edit this mask just as you can edit any other.

10 To see how the image would look without the Filter effects mask, press and hold the Shift key and click the Thumbnail of the Filter effects mask. An "X" appears and the mask is disabled. This shows how the image would look if the sharpening was applied to the entire image.

Shift+click the Filter effects mask thumbnail to disable the mask.

11 Choose File > Save, but do not close this file.

Stroking a Pen path

For special effects, or just to create an outline, you might want to stroke a path. You can follow these steps to stroke the path around the gumball machine. Keep in mind that this is just one of many ways that you can add a stroke to your image.

To use your path as a stroke, start by selecting the Brush tool and assigning a brush size, hardness, and a color. You won't just apply any stroke, but you will create your own custom brush, starting with a file that includes vector artwork.

Defining a custom brush preset

In this next section, you create your own brush preset to stroke the gumball machine with.

1   Choose File > Open and open the file in advpslessons folder named **happy brush.psd**; an image of some graphic flowers appears.

2   Select the Rectangular Marquee tool and click and drag to make a selection that surrounds the four flowers. An exact size or position is not important. Understand that the marquee you make determines the repeat of this graphic when you convert it into a brush preset.

Click and drag to make a rectangular marquee selection of the graphics.

3   Once you have a rectangular selection, choose Edit > Define Brush Preset; the Brush Name dialog box appears.

4   Type **My Brush** into the Name text field and click OK. Choose File > Close to close this file, but do not save.

Save your custom brush preset.

Editing your brush

In this next section, you will adjust the size and spacing of your custom brush before you apply it to the path.

1 Select the Brush tool and then select the Brush Preset Picker in the upper-left area of the Options bar. Scroll to the bottom of the list and make sure to select your new custom brush

2 Choose Window > Brush; your brush is already selected.

3 In the Size text field type **75**; in the Spacing text field type **120**. The spacing decides the amount of space between your brush instances.

4 Click the Create new brush icon (◼) at the bottom of the Brushes panel. The Brush name dialog box appears; name the file **My Brush edited** and click OK.

Change the size and spacing of your brush, then save it.

Applying your custom brush to the path

You will now apply the custom brush to your Pen path.

1   Create a new blank layer so you do not permanently edit your image.

2   With the Brush tool selected, press and hold the Alt (Windows) or Option (Mac OS) key to activate the eye dropper and click any Orange in the image to sample it and add it as your Foreground color.

3   Select the gum machine path in the Paths panel.

4   Select the Stroke path with brush button at the bottom of the Path's panel; your custom stroke is applied to the path.

5   Since you applied this stroke on a blank layer, you can experiment with different blending modes and opacities. In this example, Vivid light was selected from the Blending drop-down menu in the Layers panel.

The custom stroke applied to the path.

6   Choose File > Save. Keep the file open for the next part of the lesson.

Saving the image for other applications

If you are using this image in other Adobe applications, you can save it in the native Photoshop file and then choose to Place the image into the other application. By selecting File > Place, transparency is supported. If you choose to copy and paste this image, you will most likely see a white background appear in the other application.

If you want to save this image for use in an application that does not support the Photoshop format, you can choose from two main formats: PNG and EPS (which includes DCS 2.0).

PNG-24

The PNG format is a raster graphics file format that supports lossless data compression. PNG was created as an improved, non-patented replacement for Graphics Interchange Format (GIF), and is the most used lossless image compression format on graphics that appear on the screen. PNG works well for web, application assets, PowerPoint presentations, and more. Typically, PNG would not be used for documents that will be printed.

1   To save in the PNG format, choose File > Save for Web. The Save for Web dialog box appears.

2   From the Presets drop-down menu, choose PNG-24, and make sure the Transparency check box is selected.

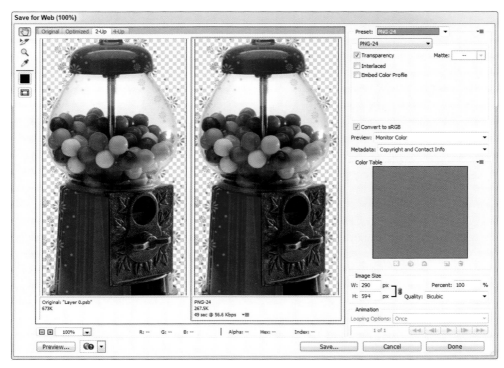

Choose the PNG-24 preset and make sure Transparency is checked.

3 Click Save at the bottom of the Save for Web dialog box.

4 In the Save Optimized As dialog box, type **advps0402_optimized**; make sure that you saving into the advps04lessons folder, and then click Save.

EPS, DCS 2.0

If you want to use transparency in documents that will be printed, you should use the EPS format. The EPS or DCS 2.0 formats can support more information and vector data. In this example, an EPS is saved.

Before saving this file, you must convert your path into a clipping path. This clipping path will define your transparency when you place the image into another application. For this lesson, you will turn off the layer that includes the stroke.

1 In the Layers panel, turn off the visibility icon (👁) on the new layer you created to apply a stroke on the path.

2 If the Paths panel is not visible, choose Windows > Path, and then select the gum machine path.

3 Click the panel menu in the Paths panel and select Clipping Path.

Convert your path into a clipping path.

4 When the Clipping Path dialog box appears, click OK.

5 Choose File Save As; the Save As dialog box appears. If necessary, type **advps0402_work**, and select Photoshop EPS from the Save as type drop-down menu. Make sure that you are saving into your advps04lesson folder and click Save; the EPS options dialog box appears.

6 In the EPS Options dialog box, make sure the Preview is set to TIFF 8 bits/pixel; this provides a preview image that is used when you place this image into other applications.

7   Check Include Vector Data and click OK.

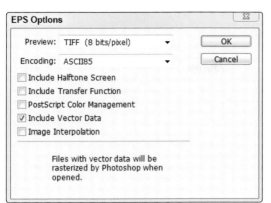

Set the EPS options.

8   Choose File > Save and then File > Close.

Self study

This lesson included intense exercises on how to control the Pen tool. Use your experience to create a path around the image named **advps0403.psd** located on your advps04lessons folder. Once you have created the path, do the following:

• Save the image in a format that supports transparency for web

• Save a clipping path

• Save in a format that supports transparency in applications other than Adobe.

Review

Questions

1   What key do you press and hold to convert a corner anchor point to curve or vice versa?

2   What tool can you use to move an entire Pen path? What tool is used to select and edit individual points or path segments in a path?

3   You import an image into an application, such as Microsoft Word, and the transparent areas appear white. What can you do resolve this issue?

Answers

1   You can convert a corner anchor point to a smooth point, or back to a corner again, by pressing and holding the Alt/Option key and clicking the anchor point when you have the Pen tool selected.

2   To move an entire path, you can select and move or even transform an entire path by using the Path Selection tool (▸) located in the Vector tools section of the Tools panel.

To select and edit individual points or path segments, you can use the Direct Selection tool to select individual path segments or points on a path. Make sure that all anchor points are deselected by clicking off the path before selecting an individual point.

3   If you import an image into another application and the transparency is not supported, you can return to the original file and save it in the PNG format. If a higher quality image is needed for printing, save in the EPS format.

Lesson 5

What you'll learn in this lesson:

- Color basics
- Reading colors using the Info panel
- Using the Curves Adjustment layer
- Painting a curve correction
- Painting filter effects

Color Correcting like a Pro

In this lesson, you'll discover the tricks used by color professionals to correct images like magic. Discover how to use curves with confidence and how to read color values. You will also find out how to take advantage of layer features to make selective color changes throughout an image.

Starting up

Before starting, make sure that your tools and panels are consistent by resetting your preferences. See "Resetting Adobe Photoshop CC preferences" in the Starting up section of this book. You will work with several files from the advps05lessons folder in this lesson. Make sure that you have loaded the advpslessons folder onto your hard drive from the supplied DVD. For more information, see "Loading lesson files" in the Starting up section of this book.

See Lesson 5 in action!

Use the accompanying video to gain a better understanding of how to use some of the features shown in this lesson. You can find the video tutorial for this lesson on the included DVD.

Understanding color

Before you can become a pro at color correcting your images, you need to understand a little about color science. You will not master everything about the science of color in this lesson, but you will be exposed to some fundamentals that will help you to know why you are making the suggested adjustments. This lesson essentially provides you with rules to follow so you can avoid making random guesses when color correcting your images.

The science of color is sometimes called chromatics, chromatography, colorimetry, or simply color science. It includes the perception of color by the human eye and brain. Making color adjustments can be inconsistent, since the color of an object depends on both the physics of the object in its environment and the characteristics of the perceiving eye and brain. To put this simply, not only does the lighting in the original location of the image have an effect on the image, but the lighting that you are working in affects your image as well. If you are working in an office environment, you might discover that you are correcting to the green cast that your fluorescent lights are producing. In addition to that, you could have a window streaming sunlight at various times of the day, producing additional color variations in your work environment. This is why this lesson is focused on reading values instead of making changes based strictly upon the visual appearance of your image.

Tools you will use

In this lesson, you will take advantage of two panels that you might not have needed in the past: the Info panel and the Histogram.

Using the Histogram panel

Understanding image histograms is probably the single most important concept to becoming familiar with Photoshop. A histogram can tell you whether your image has been properly exposed, whether the lighting is correct, and what adjustments will work best to improve your image. The histogram will also indicate whether the image has enough tonal information to produce a quality image. You will reference the Histogram panel throughout this lesson.

1 Choose File > Browse in Bridge. When Adobe Bridge appears, navigate to the advps05lessons folder that you copied onto your hard drive.

2 Locate the image named **advps0501.psd** and double-click it to open in Photoshop. An image of a tree appears. Given that the tree was not shot with professional lighting or expertise, the image offers many issues that need to be addressed.

3   Choose File > Save. In the Save As dialog box, name this file **advps0501_work** and keep it in the PSD format. Choose to save this file in the advps05lessons folder.

4   Choose Windows > Histogram to show the Histogram panel. Notice that the Histogram is rather full and spread across the span of the panel at this point.

5   Select Expanded View from the Histogram panel menu in the upper-right corner. You can now read the levels in the image as you drag your mouse across the histogram.

The original tree image.   *The original histogram.*

6   Click and drag the right side of the Histogram to see that the level values are in the 200's. The high levels on the right side of the histogram represent the lighter sections of this RGB image. Click and drag on the left side of the Histogram to see that the levels are low, indicating that this is the darkest section of the image.

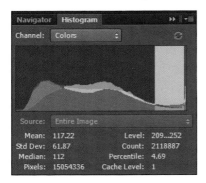

Click and drag on the Histogram to see values.

Images in the Histogram panel are represented in 255 levels or tonal values of colors. Zero (0) represents black and 255 represents white. To help you remember this concept, think about color being created with light. If you have a flashlight that is off (i.e., level 0), it is totally dark or black. If the flashlight is turned on (i.e., level 255), you have bright white.

When you start to understand that the right side of the Histogram represents the light values and the left side the dark values, it might make sense to you that, since the data in this file starts away from the edges, the image doesn't have a great amount of darks and lights. You can therefore conclude that this image is a little washed out, or lacks contrast. There is no easy formula for improving brightness and contrast, but you will use the Curves panel in this lesson to improve those aspects of your image as well.

7 Choose File > Save. Keep this file open for the next part of this lesson.

Why do Histograms look different?

Histograms will vary depending on the type of image you are viewing. Your scanner, camera's capabilities, the scene lighting, or camera settings, can all have an effect on your Histogram. There are also different types of images that you should be aware of, since they can affect the Histogram as well.

A light image is called a "high-key" image. In a high-key image, the data is heavy on the right side of the Histogram.

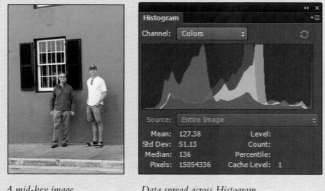

A high-key image.   *Data on the right side.*

A mid-key image spans across various levels in the Histogram.

A mid-key image.   *Data spread across Histogram.*

(continues)

Why do Histograms look different? (continued)

A low-key image would be heavy in data on the left side of the Histogram.

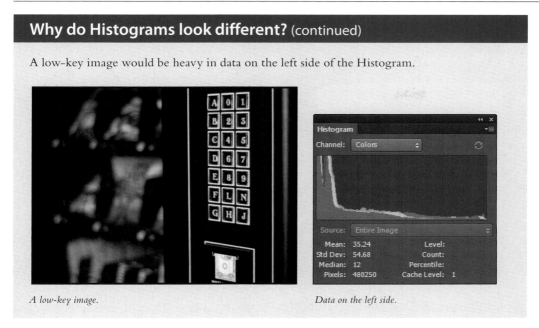

A low-key image.   *Data on the left side.*

Intentionally creating a bad Histogram reading

In this section, you will intentionally remove important data from your image. This will help you understand the effects of overworking an image, and see how those changes are reflected in the Histogram.

1   With the **advps0501_work.psd** file still open, choose Image > Adjustments > Posterize. The Posterize dialog box appears.

2   Type the value of **16** into the levels text field and click OK.

3   Now, use the Zoom tool to zoom into the leafy area of the image. Note that he values are now chopped up into 16 levels. You essentially have destroyed the nice tonal gradation from one color to another.

Tonal values before posterizing.   *Change levels to 16.*   *Image after posterizing.*

4 Take a look at your Histogram panel. If necessary, click the alert triangle symbol in the upper-right section of the panel to refresh the reading. Notice that the Histogram reflects the changes you have made by showing the tonal values spread out across all values with large spaces in-between.

The Histogram displays the poor tonal values in this image.

5 Choose File > Close, do not save changes.

You must understand that this elimination of the levels in the Histogram occurs when you make any changes to your tonal values in Photoshop. If you use Levels, then Brightness and Contrast, and then Curves, you remove important tonal information. This is why you will learn to correct color values, brightness, and contrast with the Curves panel, since it has the capability to correct all three with the minimal amount of tonal damage.

What images need to be color corrected?

Generally, images that need color correction are images that include a neutral (gray tonal values) or include skin tone. A neutral is essentially anything in the image that is gray: a shade of gray or light to dark grays. A gray value is composed of equal amounts of red, green, and blue.

The fact that gray is created from equal amounts of RGB makes it easy for viewers to notice when colors are "off". If you have an image of an orange sunset, viewers are less likely to know whether the color is accurate. A color cast could be intentional for mood, and viewers would have no reference for the original scene. On the other hand, if someone is wearing a dark suit and tie in an image, and the shirt is slightly pink, the slight pinkish color cast would be more noticeable.

In our example below, the left image is not corrected. The whites and grays in the image might look dirty or as though they have a color cast over them. The image on the right has had the grays neutralized using curves, which you will learn to do in this lesson.

Uncorrected image.   *Image with grays neutralized.*

Choosing your color settings

Many Photoshop users do not understand the importance of knowing where an image will be published; whether for print, the Web, or even a digital device like a cell phone. For this lesson, you will use generic color settings that work well for a typical print image, but you should understand the impact that color settings have on your image.

When choosing a color setting, as you will do the following lesson, you are making important decisions as to how you want your image's color adjusted for final output, or how it will look on your screen. If you are creating images that will remain on screen (i.e., for web, application or presentation view only), color settings will have less impact than if you print your image.

Importance of RGB vs. CMYK color modes

At this point, you should understand how the mode of your image is impacted by Color Settings. Settings in the Color Settings dialog box immediately change the look of your image on the screen, but do not affect the actual color values in your image until you select Image > Mode > CMYK. As long as you image remains in the RGB mode, you can continue to change your color settings to change the screen view without impacting the actual image's color values.

Understanding Gamuts

The selections in the Color Settings dialog box help you to view an image as it appears on different devices or substrates by changing the available gamut. Gamut represents the number of colors that can be represented, detected, or reproduced on a specific device. You might not realize it, but you have experience with different gamuts already; your eyes can see many more colors than your monitor or a printing press can reproduce.

Why do you use these settings? If you are using your image for in-screen presentation, you can use the options in Color Settings to see how your image will appear when viewed on the screen. If you are printing your document, you can see how the image will appear when it is printed on paper. Keep in mind that unless you are in a light controlled environment, these settings will not be perfectly accurate.

Working in the RGB mode

Unless you use an advanced color management system, you should do much of your creative work in the RGB mode. The CMYK mode is limited in its capabilities (fewer menu selections), and if you work in this mode, you have already made some Color Setting decisions that might not be accurate. Remember, as long as the image is in RGB, you can later change your settings.

1   Choose File > Open, navigate to the advps05lessons folder, and open the file named **advps0502.psd**. An image of a garden appears.

2   Choose Edit > Color Settings in Photoshop CC. The Color Settings dialog box appears.

3   As a default, North America General Purpose 2 is selected. This is a generic setting that basically indicates that Photoshop has no idea where the final output of this image will be viewed. Depending upon your image's final destination (print, web, or mobile), the results could vary widely.

4   For this example, choose North America Prepress 2. Note that all the warning check boxes become active at the bottom of the dialog box. Uncheck them for this lesson, and then click OK to exit the Color Settings dialog box. Don't worry that your Settings are now indicating Custom; this occurred because you unchecked the warnings.

Uncheck the warnings after you change the Settings.

5   To stay in the RGB mode and see the effect of your settings change, press Ctrl+Y (Windows) or Command+Y (Mac OS). This is the toggle keyboard shortcut for CMYK Preview. Using this preview, you can stay in RGB and see your image in the CMYK gamut.

You can change your preview by selecting View > Proof Setup. As a default, it is set to Working CMYK.

6   Choose File > Save As. When the Save As dialog box appears, name this file **advps0502_work**, and make sure it is in the Photoshop (PSD) format. Check to make sure that you are saving the file into the advps05lesson folder and click Save.

Note that you can adjust your color settings suite-wide by using Adobe Bridge and selecting Edit > Color Settings. Applying color settings through Adobe Bridge saves you the time and trouble of making sure that all Creative Cloud applications have the same Color Settings, and ensures that your color settings are consistent throughout your production process.

Getting a reading from the image

In this next part of the lesson, you will take a look at the garden image's existing values before you start any color correction.

Your first step will be to read the existing values using the Info panel.

1   Choose Windows > Info to open the on-screen densitometer in Photoshop.

2   Position your cursor over any of the stonework in the image, and then look at the Info panel to read the RGB values.

Position cursor over a grey area on the stonework.   *Read the values in the Info panel.*

As we mentioned earlier in this lesson, something that is gray is considered a neutral. A true neutral color is made up of equal amounts of RGB colors. If you look at your Info panel, you might see that the Red and Green are relatively close in value, but that the green is high. This could be due to numerous factors, such as the time of day or the weather. You will adjust the green later in this process.

Choosing your color settings 5

Setting a highlight and shadow

An important step in correcting an image is to make sure that you have optimal range of tonal values. In this example, you will locate the lightest and the darkest pixels in the image to create an improved tone curve. You'll set the highlight and shadow to predetermined values using the Set White Point and Set Black Point tools available in the Curves Adjustments panel. Before you begin, you'll determine what those values should be. This is a critical part of the process, since the default for the white point is 0, meaning that the lightest part of the image will have no value when printed, and any detail in this area will be lost.

Some images can get away with not having tonal values in very bright areas. Typically, reflections from metal, fire, and extremely sunlit areas, as well as reflections off other shiny objects such as jewelry, do not have value in those reflective areas.

Such areas are referred to as specular highlights. By leaving these areas without any value, the rest of the image looks balanced and the shine pops out of the image. Good examples of objects that could contain specular highlights are jewelry, candlelight, or metal.

This image has specular highlights, which should be left with a value of zero.

Lesson 5, Color Correcting like a Pro   125

Locating the white and black point

Before you get started, you will change a simple preference to make it easier for you to interpret the Curves Adjustment panel. In this part of the lesson, you will take advantage of the Threshold feature to easily find the lightest and darkest parts in the image. Threshold allows you to reduce a multi-tonal image into just two values: white and black.

1 Choose Image > Adjustment > Threshold; the Threshold dialog box appears.

2 Click and drag the Threshold slider to the right and notice that in the preview, the lightest colors in the image remain white, while the darker parts of the image change to a solid black. Continue dragging the slider over to the right until you barely see any white; this is the lightest part of your image. Do not click OK; leave the Threshold dialog box open while you take the next steps.

3 Press and hold the Shift key and click in the light area of your image. By Shift+clicking, you have created a color sample at the location in which you clicked. This step does not change the image, but leaves a marker that you can refer to later.

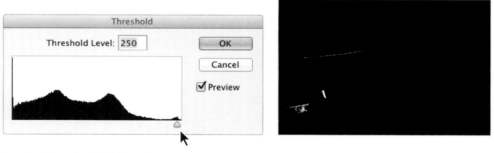

Drag the slider in the Threshold panel to the right.   *Shift+click the lightest part of the image.*

4 Now drag the Threshold slider to the left. Notice that the darkest parts of the image remain black while the light parts preview as white. Do not drag the entire way to the left, since you will then only be left with the dark woods. Your goal is to find the darkest area in this image that is in the main focal point of the image: the garden.

5 Shift+click the darkest section of this image to create a second color sample.

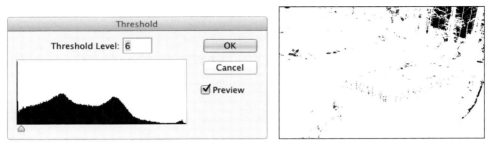

Drag the slider in the Threshold panel to the left.   *Shift+click the lightest part of the image.*

You can press and hold the Shift key and click and drag a color sample to reposition it.

6 Note that you must click Cancel in the Threshold dialog box. If you accidently click OK, press Ctrl+Z (Windows) or Command+Z (Mac OS) to undo the Threshold change and keep your color samples.

You can create up to four color samplers in your image at a time. Color samplers help you refer back to an exact location in your image. You will use the color samplers to help you locate and set the highlights and shadows in this image, as well as read other values. If you need to remove any color sampler, you can select the Color Sampler tool ( ), which is hidden in the Eyedropper tool, and then press and hold the Alt (Windows) or Option (Mac OS) key while you click the color sampler.

Now that you have determined where you lightest point and darkest point in the image are, you will use them to improve the tonal values of this image.

Defining highlight and shadow

The process of defining values for the highlight (lightest) and shadow (darkest) in your image is not difficult, but it helps to know where the image will be used. If you have a good relationship with a printer, they can tell you the white point (lightest) or black point (darkest) values that work best for their presses and material that they will print on. Alternatively, you can use the generic values suggested in this book. The values shown in this example are good for typical printing setups and for screen display.

1 If your Layers panel is not visible, select Window > Layers.

2 With **advps0502_work.psd** open, click the Create new fill or adjustment layer button (⬤) and select Curves; the Properties panel with Curves appears.

3 Double-click the Sample in image to set the white point button (𝒫) found on the left side of the Curves Adjustments panel; the Color Picker (Target Highlight Color) dialog box appears. Even though you are in the RGB mode, you can set values in any of the color environments displayed in this window. In this example, you'll use CMYK values.

4 Type **5** in the C (Cyan) text field, **3** in the M (Magenta) text field and **3** in the Y (Yellow) text field. Leave K (Black) at 0, and click OK. A warning dialog box appears asking whether you would like to save the target values; click Yes.

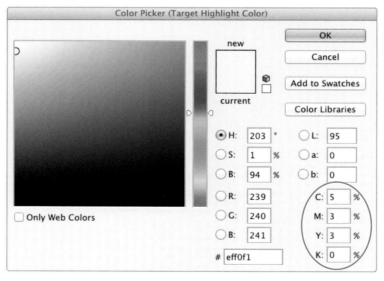

Setting the target highlight color.

If you have properly defined your Color Settings, you should not need to change the Set black point values. If you have a close relationship with a printer, and they are supplying you with their maximum black values, you could double-click the Sample in image to set the Black Point eyedropper (✐) and enter the values that they have provided.

Selecting the black point eyedropper.

After all this setup, you still need to adjust your image. The good news is that you do not have to set up each separate image once you've done this initial set up.

5 Select Sample in image to set the white point eyedropper (✐), and click the #1 color sampler you placed earlier. By clicking the color sampler you had defined in this area of the image as the lightest point on the tone curve, you are adjusting the image to the newly defined highlight color values.

If this gives you unexpected results, it could be because you missed the color sampler. You can undo by pressing Ctrl+Z (Windows) or Command+Z (Mac OS). Try clicking again.

Now you will set the black, or darkest, part of your image.

6 Make sure that the Sample in image to set black point eyedropper is selected, and then click the #2 color sampler that you added earlier. This has now been set as the darkest area of the image, using the values you input earlier in this example.

You should already see a slight difference in the image (a slight color cast has been applied) but you are not done yet.

7 Leave the Curves Properties panel visible for the next exercise.

Adjusting the midtones

In many cases, you need to lighten the midtones (middle values of an image) to make details more apparent in the image.

1   Select the center (midtone area) of the white curve line and drag upward slightly to lighten the image in the midtones. This is the only visual correction that you will make to this image. You want to be careful that you do not adjust too much, since you can lose valuable information.

A. Three-quarter tones. *B.* Midtones.
C. Quarter tones.

2 Add a little contrast to your image by clicking the three-quarter tone area of the white curve line (the area between the middle of the curve and the top, as shown in the figure), then clicking and dragging down slightly. Again, this is a visual correction, so don't make too drastic a change.

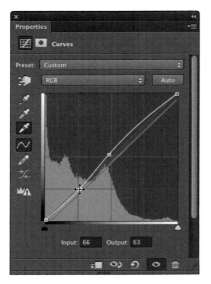

Click and drag the three-quarter tone
up slightly to lighten the image.

3 Keep the Curves Properties panel open for the next section of this lesson.

In this next part of the lesson, you will choose to neutralize this image. Although there are many automatic tools that you can use in Photoshop to neutralize an image, you will make the steps manually. This will help you to better understand what you are doing and lead you into more advanced corrections.

Balancing the neutrals in an image

In this next part of the process, you will use the gray stones in the image as a ruler to check the gray balance. As mentioned earlier in this lesson, reading a gray value helps you measure color, since a neutral gray is composed of equal amounts of red, green, and blue. Knowing this allows you to adjust for color inaccuracies.

1 With the **advps0502_work.psd** file still open, position your cursor over the gray sidewalk on the right side of the image and Shift+click to add a color sampler at this spot. A #3 color sampler appears.

As mentioned earlier in this lesson, the values in the Info panel indicate that the neutrals in this image are not balanced. You will now discover what to do with that information.

Shift+click the sidewalk.

Note that in the Info panel a third color Sampler has been added. Note also that there are two sets of values separated by a backslash (/). The values on the left side of the backslash are the values the image had before any curves adjustments were made. The values after the backslash are the values based on the changes you recently made: setting the highlight and shadow.

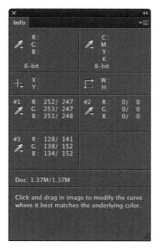

A third color sampler is added.

You will now make a manual adjustment on the curve to balance the image. Your values are likely different than the example shown in this book, but you should still be able to follow along using your own values.

2   In this example, you see that Red is a lower value than Green and Blue. Your values might vary, depending upon where you clicked, but should be proportionally the same.

If your values are all different, look at the Info panel and locate the middle value for #3. Then follow the next steps to adjust the other colors values up or down to meet that middle value. (In other words, leave the middle value intact, and adjust the other two values to closely match it.)

3   Return to the Curves Properties panel, and from the RGB drop-down menu, select Red.

4   Click the Click and drag in image button () in the upper-left area of the Curves Properties panel.

5   Position your cursor over the #3 sampler you placed on the sidewalk in the image; press and hold the Alt (Windows) or Option (Mac OS) key and click. This adds an anchor point to your Red curve and indicates where on the curve that value is located.

6   Click the newly created anchor point and drag straight up while watching the second set of values in the Info panel. Drag up until the Red values are close to the Green values.

If your values are within 1–2 values, you do not have to make these steps to adjust them.

Select Red from the Curves drop-down menu.

If you ever work on an image with three separate values you would follow the same steps, leaving the middle value in intact and dragging the other two colors to match it.

7   Review how your image looked before your adjustment by clicking the visibility eye (👁) icon to the left of the Curves 1 layer in your Layers panel.

You can add anchor points to your curve by just clicking the curve. This might be necessary if you have to balance and image in several locations. You can delete an anchor point from a curve by clicking the anchor point and dragging it off the curve.

Adding additional curve corrections

In this next step, you will add an additional curve correction to lighten some of the darker areas in the image without changing the overall curve correction you just made.

1   Using your Lasso tool, select the dark area of the garden on the right side of the image. No exact selection is necessary.

2   Click the Create new fill or adjustment layer button (●) at the bottom of the Layers panel and choose Curves.

3   Click in the middle of the Curve in the Curves Properties panel and drag up to lighten that section of the image. Notice that there is a hard edge to this selection; fix it with feathering as shown in the next step.

Click and drag up to lighten the selection.   *Note that only your selection is changed.*

4   Click the Masks icon located at the top of the Properties panel to see your selection options.

5   Click and drag the Feather slider to the right until you have successfully removed the hard edge and blended your curve change in the image. In this example, the feathering is set to **30 px**.

You can feather the mask for the adjustment layer at any time.

Notice that your mask is shown in the Curves 2 layer in the Layers panel. You can also see that your image is affected wherever there is white on the mask.

6   Select the Paint Brush tool and press **D** to make sure that your foreground color is white and your background color is black.

You can switch foreground and background colors by pressing **X**.

7   Position your cursor out on the image so that you can see a preview of the brush size. If you see a crosshair instead of a circular preview of your brush size, you most likely have your Caps Lock key on; turn it off to see the brush preview.

8   Press the right bracket key (]) repeatedly until you have a brush that is a larger. No exact size is necessary.

9 Now press and hold the Shift key and press the Left Bracket ([) repeatedly to soften the brush. (You can also select the Brush preset button in the Paint Brush options bar and set the size to approximately 40 px and the Hardness to 0%.)

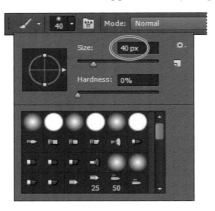

Brush size is approximately 40 px with 0% hardness.

10 Start painting the image where you have other dark areas to correct the image by painting it. Notice that you expose the curve correction wherever you paint with white on the mask. If you take a look at the mask, you will see that a white patch has been added where you painted.

Paint your curve correction.

11 Now press **5** to change the opacity of the Paint Brush tool to 50%. Start painting other parts of the image that you want to lighten; notice that the curve adjustment is only applied at a 50% level where you paint. If you were to continue to paint over those areas, you would eventually build up the Opacity to 100%.

Paint with various opacities.

Adding more variation to your curve adjustment

The goal of this exercise is for you to see how you can take painting curve adjustments on your image even further. You will now edit your changes even more by painting with black.

1 Press **X** to switch your background and foreground colors. Your foreground color should now be black.

2 Press **25** to set your opacity to 25%, and then start painting over some of the areas that you have already lightened. Notice that you are undoing the curve change that you had made previously, but only a bit at a time. If you keep releasing the Paint Brush tool and painting over the same area, you would eventually build up to 100% black and no curves adjustment would be made in that area.

3 Experiment by pressing **X** to switch to a white foreground color and then paint to lighten another area of the image. Press **X** again to change your foreground color to black and erase some of the adjustment that you made. As you are painting, notice the changes that are being applied to your Layer mask thumbnail in the Layers panel.

As you paint on the mask, you can see changes.

4 Choose File > Save. Keep this image open for the next part of this lesson.

Sharpening the image

In this next section, you will take all three layers that you have been working with and convert them into a Smart layer. You will then adjust the sharpness of the image.

1   Select the Background layer in the Layers panel and then Shift+click the two curves adjustment layers that you added earlier in this lesson. All three layers are selected.

2   Right-click (Windows) or Ctrl+click (Mac OS) the right side of any of those layers and select Convert to Smart Object. All three layers are reduced down to one combined Smart Object layer called Curves 2, the name of the topmost layer.

Select all three layers and convert into one Smart Object.

3   Choose View > 100%. Note that you must be at 100% view when applying filters in Photoshop; otherwise, you might see strange effects caused by the resolution of your screen.

4   Choose Filter > Sharpen > UnSharp Mask. Although there are many different sharpening features from which to select, this feature gives you access to the manual features you need to create a professional sharpening effect on your image.

5 When the UnSharp mask dialog box appears, click and drag the slider to the right until you reach **500%**. Obviously, this is sharpening the image too much and you start to see some artifacting in the image.

Example of sharpening: image of child vs. senior

The amount of sharpening that you apply depends on the subject matter. If you have a product image, you can sharpen it more than an image of a person. Even people tend to work well with different settings; a child can have more sharpening applied than someone later in age, for instance.

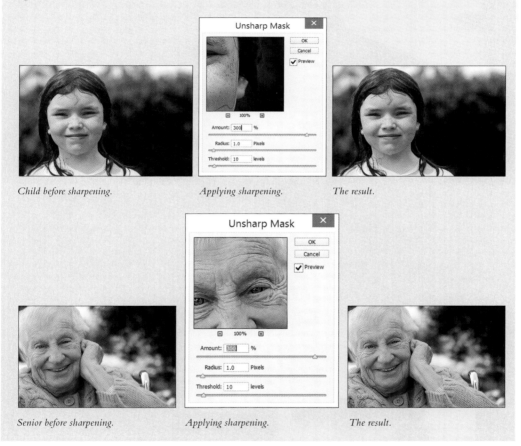

Child before sharpening.   *Applying sharpening.*   *The result.*

Senior before sharpening.   *Applying sharpening.*   *The result.*

6 Change the Amount value to **150%**, since this value works well for the garden scene.

7 Leave the Radius at **1.0**. Photoshop creates a small halo around parts of your image where it sees a contrast; this is something you do not want to make too apparent.

8   Most importantly, change the Threshold to **10**. This indicates to Photoshop that, if the contrast of pixels that are next to each other is within 10 levels (think of shades) of each other, they are not an edge and should not be sharpened. If the contrast is higher, the unsharp masking is applied; otherwise, those areas are ignored, thereby reducing noise or graininess in your image.

Adjust the settings for UnSharp Mask.

9   Click OK. Note that since you created a Smart Object, a Smart Filter is applied. A Filter effects layer appears in your Layers panel, along with a mask called the Filter effects thumbnail mask.

A. *Filter effects.* **B.** *Filter effects thumbnail mask.*
C. *Blending Options.*

Painting your filter on your image

In this next part of the lesson, you will paint sharpness on your image by taking advantage of the Filter effects thumbnail mask.

1   Click the Filter effects thumbnail and press **D** to make sure that you are using the default foreground and background colors. Press **X** to make sure that black is your foreground color.

2   Select the Paint Brush tool (✐) and then press **0** (zero) to make sure that your Paint Brush is back to 100% Opacity.

3   Start painting over a section of the image. Note that the unsharp mask is no longer applied wherever you paint black.

4   With the Filter effects thumbnail still selected, choose Edit > Fill. Choose **Black**, **Normal** mode, **100%** Opacity, and then click OK. Your entire Filter effects thumbnail is filled with black and no unsharp masking is applied.

5   Press **X** to switch your foreground color to white and start painting. Note that you are now sharpening the image only where you choose to.

You can paint white and black at varying opacities to paint your filter.

6   Experiment by changing the opacity value of your brush as you did when you edited the Curves adjustment layer's mask. Notice that you have total control, in a painterly fashion, to change how sharpness is applied to your image.

Adjusting the Blending of the filter

Sometimes, when you apply sharpening to an image, some artifacting appears in the form of speckles. You can avoid this effect by sharpening only the grays in an image instead of all the color pixels. In this next part of the lesson, you will find out how to change your Filter blend mode to Luminosity, which will change the Unsharp mask to apply only to the neutrals in your image.

1 With the **advps02_work.psd** file still open, double-click the Double-click to edit filter blending options icon in the Layers panel (▤). The Blending Options dialog box appears.

2 From the Mode drop-down menu, select Luminosity and click OK. You might not see a difference in this particular image, but try this on some of your own images to see whether they appear to have specks of color throughout.

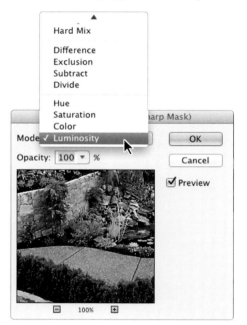

Change the blend mode to Luminosity.

3 Choose File > Save and File > Close.

Self study

Open any image that contains a neutral. Keep in mind that a neutral is any shade of gray. Some good images that you can use to practice color correction on your own should contain someone wearing a white or gray shirt, or an image with a gray road, white building, etc.

Many photographers purchase gray cards and place them near their subjects when shooting images. The photographers then use that gray to balance the image and crop it out of the final image.

Start by looking at your Info panel. Can you see whether the gray are balanced, or do they need some adjustment? If an adjustment is necessary, follow the steps in this lesson to change the image.

Review

Questions

1 What is a color gamut?

2 What is a neutral gray?

3 How can you paint a filter effect only where you want in an image?

Answers

1 A color gamut is the number of colors that can be represented, detected, or reproduced on a specific device.

2 A neutral gray is composed of equal amounts of red, green, and blue.

3 You can paint a filter effect only where you want by selecting the Filter effects thumbnail and painting on it.

Lesson 6

What you'll learn in this lesson:

- Using the content-aware tools
- Combining images
- Adjusting the tonal values
- Using the Clone tool

Painting and Retouching

In this lesson, you will discover how to manipulate the pixels in your image to create realistic retouching.

Starting up

Before starting, make sure that your tools and panels are consistent by resetting your preferences. See "Resetting Adobe Photoshop CC preferences" in the Starting up section of this book. You will work with several files from the advps06lessons folder in this lesson. Make sure that you have loaded the advpslessons folder onto your hard drive from the supplied DVD. For more information, see "Loading lesson files" in the Starting up section of this book.

See Lesson 6 in action!

Use the accompanying video to gain a better understanding of how to use some of the features shown in this lesson. You can find the video tutorial for this lesson on the included DVD.

Content Painting tools

In this lesson, you will use a variety of the healing and retouching tools available in Photoshop to improve an image. In addition to the healing and retouching tools, you will activate an additional option, called Content-Aware, that allows the tools to be cognizant of the pixels surrounding your selection.

The Content-Aware features dramatically simplify the process of removing objects from an image or even expanding the boundaries of a cropped image. You will have an opportunity to take advantage of the capabilities in this lesson.

Retouching an image

In this part of the lesson, you will take an amateur shot and use the retouching tools to remove unwanted elements from the image and improve the lighting. You will start by opening the finished image.

1   Choose File > Open, navigate to the advps06lesson folder, and open the image named **advps0601_done**. An image of a frog appears. Choose Windows > Layers to see that quite a bit of work has been done to this image to improve its appearance. You can keep this file open for reference or close it now. Next, you will open your start file.

2   Navigate to the advps06lesson file folder and open **advps0601.psd**; an image of a frog appears. The image has some elements in it, such as the blade of grass that should be removed.

The original frog image.

3 Choose File > Save As. When the Save As dialog box appears, type **advps0601_work** into the File Name text field and make sure that you have the destination folder advps06lessons selected. Confirm that the format is Photoshop, and then click Save.

4 Double-click Background in the Layers panel; the New Layer dialog box appears. In the Name text field, type **Frog Original** and click OK.

New Layer	
Name: Frog Original	OK
☐ Use Previous Layer to Create Clipping Mask	Cancel
Color: ☒ None	
Mode: Normal Opacity: 100 %	

Naming the layer.

Repositioning the branch

The first step in your retouching exercise involves moving the foreground branch away from the frog's face to expose the snout. You will then eliminate the distracting blade of grass. Before starting, you will extend the image canvas to the right by increasing the canvas size using the Crop tool. Note that you can use the Crop tool not just to crop images, but also to extend an image's canvas by adjusting the handles.

1 Press **C** to select the Crop tool (⌗). Transformation handles appear around the four corners of the crop area and also in the center of each side.

2 From the Crop tool presets drop-down menu in the Options bar, confirm that your selection is set to Ratio.

3 If you do not see rulers in your workspace press Ctrl+R (Windows) or Command+R (Mac OS) to display the rulers. Right-click (Windows) or Ctrl+click (Mac OS) the actual ruler to open a contextual menu and confirm or change your values to Inches.

4   Click and drag the transformation handle in the center of the right side towards the right until the center target in the crop area is about equal distance between the nostril and snout, or until you have reached about the 14.5-15 inch area in your ruler. Click the Commit button in the upper-right of the Options bar, or press Enter (Windows) or Return (Mac OS) to commit the crop. A transparent canvas area has been added to the image.

Using the Crop tool to add canvas area to the image.

5   You will now duplicate this layer to keep an unedited version. Click and drag the Frog layer down to the Create new layer button (⬛) in the Layers panel. A new layer named Frog Original copy is created.

6   Hide the Frog Original layer by clicking the corresponding visibility eye icon in the layer stack.

Duplicating a layer.

7   Select the Lasso tool (◯). You will set the feather (vignette) value before you make the selection.

When selecting a feathered amount, you can choose the setting before you create a selection. You can also choose the setting afterwards using Refine Edge in the Options bar.

8 In the Lasso tool Options bar, type **2** into the Feather text field, and then click and draw around the stick and entire right side of the image. Don't worry about the end of the nose at this point.

Creating the feathered selection.

Creating a new layer from the selection

You will now create a new layer for the selected content, and then move the content to the right. The method you will use lifts the selection up and off the original layer onto its own new layer.

1 Press Ctrl+Shift+J (Windows) or Command+Shift+J (Mac OS). This cuts the selection from the current layer and creates a new layer.

2 Select the Move tool (⊕), and then press and hold the Shift key while you move the selection to the right. By pressing and holding the Shift key, you keep the selection in alignment.

3   Double-click the new layer's name (Layer 1) and rename the layer to **Right Side**. Choose File > Save to save your work.

Move the image content to the right side of the image.

4   In the Layers panel, press and hold the Alt (Windows) or Option (Mac OS) key, and then click the Create new layer button (▣). The New Layer dialog box appears.

5   In the Name text field, type **black background**, and then click OK. A new layer is created on top of your Right Side layer.

Add a new blank layer.

6   Press the **D** key to reset your foreground and background colors back to their default of black and white.

7   Press Alt+Backspace (Windows) or Option+Delete (Mac OS) to automatically fill the black background layer with black.

8   Move this layer down in the layer stack to just above frog original. You can do this by dragging the black background layer with the Move tool (⊹). You can also move the layer down by selecting the layer, pressing and holding the Ctrl key (Windows) or Command key (Mac OS), and pressing the [(left bracket) key twice.

Fill with the background color.

Adding an adjustment layer

You will now add some contrast and mute the colors slightly.

1   Select the layer called Right Side, click and hold the Create new Fill and Adjustment layer icon, and select Black and White. The Properties panel displays the options for the Black and White adjustment, and the default black and white setting is applied to the image.

2   Using the Blending Mode drop-down menu from the Layers panel, change the mode from normal to Soft Light.

3 From the Properties Preset drop-down menu, select High Contrast Red Filter. Next, you will darken the Right Side layer, since its brightness is quite dominant now.

Creating the black and white adjustment.

Changing the Layer Properties.

4 Click the Right Side layer, and then select Curves from the Create New Fill or Adjustment layer button (●) at the bottom of the Layers panel. The Properties panel now displays the Curves adjustment options.

Create a new curve adjustment.

5 Position the cursor so that it is midway between the new Curves 1 layer and the Right Side layer. Press and hold the Alt key (Windows) or Option key (Mac OS), and click the horizontal line between the two layers. When you see the downward facing arrow and square icon, click. You have just grouped the adjustment layer (Curves 1) with the Right Side layer, so any adjustments you make to these two layers will not affect the layers beneath. Grouping layers in this way is called creating a clipping group, and it essentially turns the lower layer into a mask for the adjustment layer.

Creating a clipping group.

6   In the Properties panel, position your cursor so that it is in the top-right position of the diagonal, and then click and drag down to just below the halfway point on the curve. This action darkens the layer by selecting the lighter tones and reducing their luminance values. Next, you will darken the midtones in this image.

Reducing the brightness in the image using Curves.

7   As expected, the midtone area in curves is in the middle of the curve. Click the curve at about the halfway point and drag it down slightly. No definite amount is necessary.

8   Double-click the Frog Original copy layer and rename it to **left side**.

Lowering the midtones.

Adding a vector mask

In this next section, you will paint on the of the Right Side layer.

1   Make sure that you have the Right Side layer selected, and click the Add layer mask icon (▣) at the bottom of the layer panel.

2   Select your Paint Brush by pressing the **B** key, then right-click the canvas to bring up the brush selection menu. Choose a soft round brush (Hardness 0% and Opacity 50%) and paint out some of the hard edges. Now that the right side is looking better, it's time to look at the left side.

Softening the edges.

3   Next stage is to soften the left side layer's edge. Using the same technique as with the Right Side layer, create a new mask, and using a soft brush, paint around the sharp edges.

Softening the left side.

Retouching the frog's nose

Now you will work on the frog's nose. You will start by opening up a different file from your lessons folder.

1 Choose File > Open, and from the advps06lessons folder, open the image called **frog_2.tif**, an image of the frog appears.

2 Select the Lasso tool ($\wp$), reset your feather value to **0px**, and then click and drag a selection around the nose.

Selecting the nose.

3 Press Ctrl+C (Windows) or Command+C (Mac OS) to copy this selection. Return to the **advps0601_work.psd** image, and then press Ctrl+V (Windows) or Command+V (Mac OS) to paste the layer.

4 Return to the **frog_2.tif** image and choose File > Close.

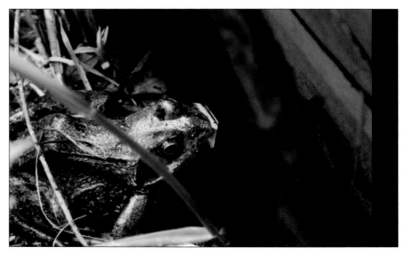

Pasting into the main document.

5   Double-click the name Layer 1 to change this layer's name to **nose**.

Paste the new nose.

6   Select the Move tool (✛) and then press **5** to lower the Opacity of this layer to 50%. You are lowering the Opacity so you can align the layers a little easier, but will return this layer to its full opacity after the next step.

Reduce the opacity of the layer to 50%.

7   With the Move tool (▶⊹), click and drag the nose to reposition it. The goal is to get a relatively good match with the left side layer. Once you achieve this, press **0** to return the layer to 100% opacity.

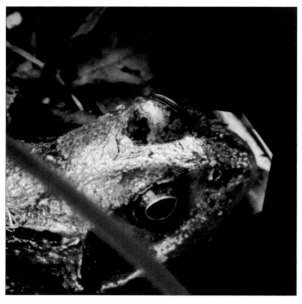

Aligning the new nose.

8   Double-click the Zoom tool (🔍) to change the view of your image to 100%.

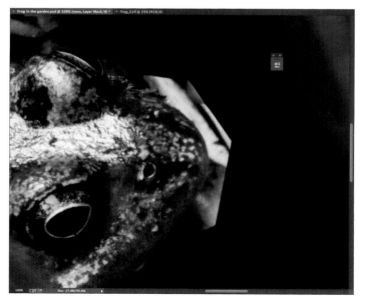

Change the view of the image.

9 With the nose layer still selected, click the Add a layer mask button (⬛) at the bottom of the Layers panel. A layer mask thumbnail appears to the right of your nose layer.

10 Select the Paint Brush tool (✐), and then right-click the canvas. This opens the Brush preset context menu. Scroll down the list of brushes until you can select Chalk 11 pixels.

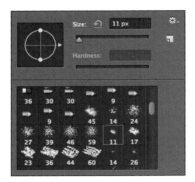

Selecting the brush.

11 Press the] (right bracket) key 8 times to increase the brush size to approximately 50 pixels, and then paint around the frog's nose to blend it in.

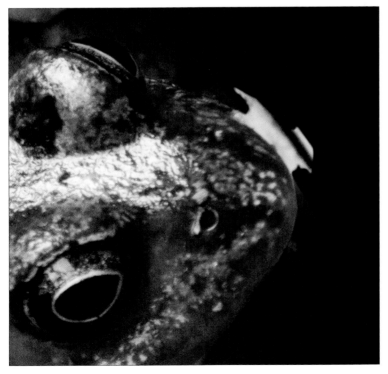

Masking the nose to blend it in.

12 Select the nose layer, and add select Curves from the Add a new fill or adjustment layer button (●) at the bottom of the Layers panel.

Removing the window.

13 To blend the nose layer with the rest of the frog, click and drag the top-right section of the curve down about a third of the amount, or until the Output value is about 175.

If you do not see the Input and Output values, click and drag down the bottom of the Properties panel to expose the bottom section of the panel.

Lowering the white point to match the tone of underlying layers.

Organizing your Layers panel

You will now organize your layers panel. You will start by selecting multiple layers and putting them into a Layer group.

1 With the nose layer still selected, Shift+click in the Curves 2 layer, and the left side layer, and then press Ctrl+G (Windows) or Command+G (Mac OS) to group the layers together into a folder.

Group your layers together to better organize your files.

2 Double–click the Group name and type **left side**.

Renaming the group left side.

3 Now select the Right Side layer and the Curves 1 layer that is above that layer and press Ctrl+G (Windows) or Command+G (Mac OS) to group those layers together.

4 Double-click the newly created group name and type **right side**.

Create a second layer group named right side.

Using the Clone Stamp tool

In this section, you will have the opportunity to use the Clone Stamp tool for retouching.

1 Click the arrow on the left side to open the left side folder.

2 Press and hold the Alt/Option key and click the Create new layer icon (◼) at the bottom of the Layers panel. When the New Layer dialog box appears, type **clean up** and click OK. You will use this layer now for retouching.

Clean up layer.

3 Select the Clone Stamp tool (♨) and click the Brush Preset picker in the Options bar to open the Brush settings. Use the slider to change the size of the Clone Stamp tool to **250** pixels.

4   Also in the Options bar, select Current & Below from the Sample drop-down menu. This will then clone what is in your current layer as well as pixels from the layers below. You will now define a source for your clone Stamp tool.

Clone stamp brush.

5   Press and hold the Alt (Windows) or Option (Mac OS) key and click just off the right of the blade of grass. This has now been designated as the source, or starting point, for your Clone Stamp tool.

6   Position the cursor over the grass to see a preview of what you will paint appear. Start painting with the Clone Stamp tool. Also notice that a cross-hair cursor appears where you originally Alt/Option-clicked, showing you the pixels that you are presently cloning. Paint over the grass until you have removed as much as you can without painting over the frog.

Removing the grass.

7 Using the Brush preset picker in the Clone Stamp options, change the brush size to about **100** px.

8 Select the Zoom tool (🔍) and click the image to zoom in closer. Go through the same process across the frog, starting with areas that define form, such as across the back, the crease in the back leg, and around the back of the eye.

To minimize the telltale repetition signs of clone stamping, use as big a brush as you can and keep sampling from different areas to break the pattern up. If you can find usable texture, color, and tone from another part of the image, use it. For example, the area behind the eye could be used for the area in front of the eye as your source. Blend it in with a bit of clone-stamping using the area behind the front leg as your source.

Stage 1 cloning — using areas on the back as source points.

Stage 2 cloning — using areas of tonal contrast to define form.

Stage 3 cloning — rebuilding a leg.

9 Continue retouching with the clone Stamp tool until the blade of grass is removed.

To maintain a convincing look, use sample areas that match the direction of light to the area you're painting over.

Blade of grass removed.

10 Now that the grass has been cleared from the frog, click the left side layer and select the Burn tool (🔍), which is about two-thirds of the way down your Tools panel (grouped with the Dodge tool and the Sponge tool). Looking at the Options bar change the Range option to Midtones and the Exposure to 20%.

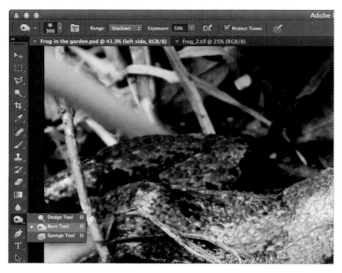

Selecting the Burn tool.

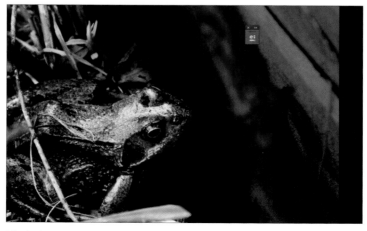

Adjusting the settings.

11 If it helps, adjust the brush size to about 125 pixels and then begin painting around the top of the back leg to darken down the background grass. At this low an exposure, setting it correctly will take a few a few brush strokes to gradually get to the level of tone required.

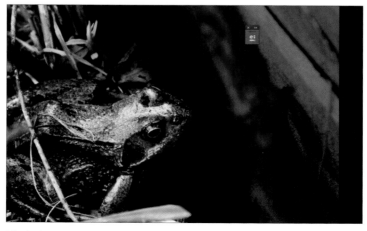

The final image.

12 For a final tweak, select the right side group and the Move tool (⊹). Clicking anywhere on the canvas while pressing and holding the Shift key, drag the right side group slightly across and to the left.

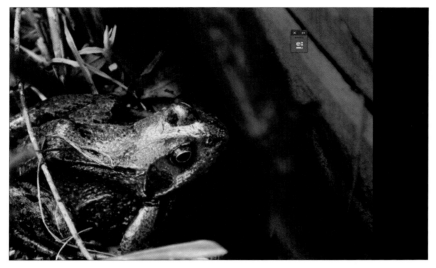

A final compositional move.

13 Press and hold the Ctrl (Windows) or Command (Mac OS) key, and then click the Frog Original layer. This activates the layer as a selection. You will use this selection to crop the image.

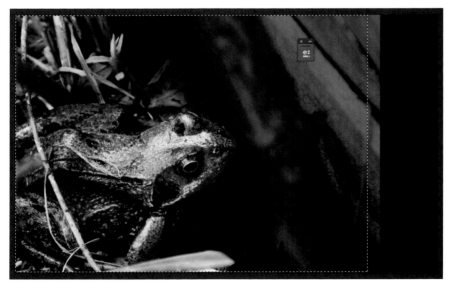

Creating a selection of the layer.

14 Select Image > Crop; the image is cropped to your selection size.

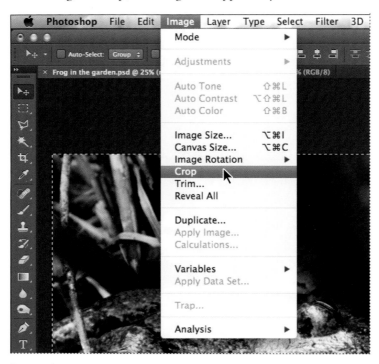

Cropping the image.

Adding a vignette

Now for a final touch, you'll add a vignette to this image.

1 Select the Black & White 1 layer, press and hold the Alt/Option key, and click the Create new layer button (◼) at the bottom of the layers panel.

2 In the New Layer dialog box, type **vignette** into the Name text field, and then click OK.

3 Press **D** to make sure that you are back to the default black and white foreground and background colors, and then press Ctrl+Backspace (Windows) or Command+Delete (Mac OS) to fill the background with White.

4   From the Blending mode drop-down menu in the Layers panel, select Multiply.

Setting up the vignette.

5   Choose Filter > Lens Correction; the Lens Correction dialog box appears. Using Lens correction you can fix common lens flaws such as barrel and pincushion distortion, vignetting, and chromatic aberration. You can also use to create an interesting effect for our vignette, as you will do in this section.

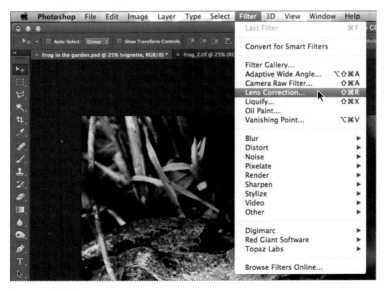

Lens correction filter.

6   Click the Custom tab and in the Vignette section (middle), slide the Amount slider to the left until it reaches –100, and then click OK.

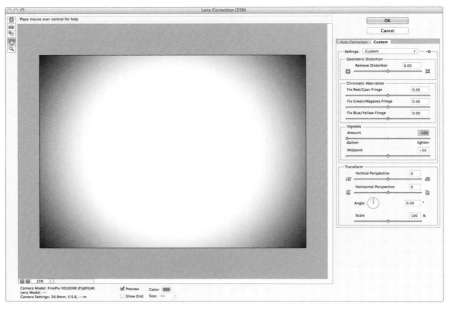

The full vignette.

7   Your image is now complete. Choose File > Save, and then File > Close.

Self study

There are times when you want an element in your image to have the appearance of being behind another object. For example, you may want to make it look like a ribbon is wrapped around an object, or that a barn is behind a wheat field. To easily create these effects you can use layer techniques. Try this technique with an image that has been included in your advps06lessons folder, **advps0603.psd**. On your own, select the ribbon that is wrapped around the package. Only select the area that will cover the stems of the flowers and press Ctrl+J (Windows) or Command+J (Mac OS) to lift that section of ribbon to its own layer. Then drag that newly created layer to the top of the stacking order to create the appearance of the dried flowers being tied under the ribbon.

Review

Questions

1   What is an easy method you can use to help you align one layer with another?

2   What are two main benefits to using an adjustment layer when retouching an image?

3   Why would you create a clipping group when using adjustment layers?

Answers

1   Sometimes you need to manually align your layers, and way of doing this easily is to change the opacity of one the layers you want to align. When your Move tool is selected, change the Opacity by typing a value. For instance, if you type **5**, the selected layer now has 50% Opacity; type **45**, and now it is at 45% Opacity. You can then align your layers and press 0 (zero) to return to 100% when you're done.

2   The benefit of using an adjustment layer when retouching an image is that you can make changes to your adjustment as long as the layer is not flattened into the rest of the image, and also that you can essentially paint your adjustment by taking advantage of the adjustment layer mask.

3   When using adjustment layers, the adjustment is reflected in all the layers that are under it in the stacking order. Creating a clipping group by right-clicking the layer and selecting Create Clipping Mask, or by pressing and holding the Alt/Option key as you click the dividing line between two layers, lets you make a mask of the bottommost layer and prevent the adjustment from affecting any other layers beneath.

What you'll learn in this lesson:

- Using Smart Objects
- Applying Smart Filters
- Using Masks in your composition
- Color grading an image

Creating Compositions

In this lesson, you will discover an approach to compositing images from multiple sources. You will find out how to use Smart Objects, Smart Filters, and masks to create an interesting final image.

Starting up

Before starting, make sure that your tools and panels are consistent by resetting your preferences. See "Resetting Adobe Photoshop CC preferences" in the Starting up section of this book. You will work with several files from the advps07lessons folder in this lesson. Make sure that you have loaded the advpslessons folder onto your hard drive from the supplied DVD. For more information, see "Loading lesson files" in the Starting up section of this book.

See Lesson 7 in action!

Use the accompanying video to gain a better understanding of how to use some of the features shown in this lesson. You can find the video tutorial for this lesson on the included DVD.

Reviewing Smart Objects

Throughout this book, you have been using Smart Objects to create many of the images included in the exercises.

You have discovered that Smart Objects can be scaled, edited, updated, and even replaced, since they represent a placed instance of your smart layer. Essentially, you embed an original copy of your selected layer or layers, then convert the layer to a Smart Object. As long as the Smart Object exists and is not flattened, you can return to that original image content at any time.

Applying Smart Filters

When you apply a filter to a Smart Object, the filter is considered a Smart Filter. Smart Filters work like regular filters, but offer you the ability to make changes to settings, opacity, and blending effects. You can access Smart Filters by applying a filter to a Smart Object, or you can choose the Filter > Convert to Smart Filter menu item.

In this lesson, you will take some images and combine them to create an interesting composition. You will also have the opportunity to take advantage of Smart Filters along the way.

1   Choose File > New. Select the International Paper from the Preset drop-down menu and then make sure that A4 is selected for the size. Type **Street Scene Comp** into the Name text field and click OK.

New document settings.

2   Navigate to the advps07lessons folder and double-click to open **street.psd**. Notice that a layer is already masked for you.

3 Right-click the straightened layer and click Convert to Smart Object.

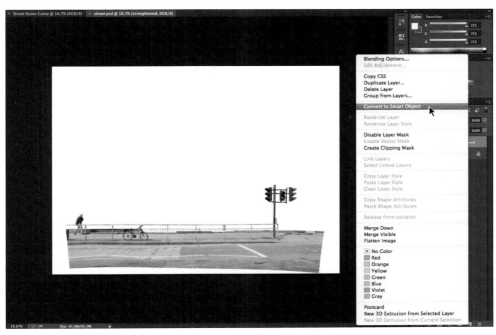

Converting layer to Smart Object

Next, you will drag the newly created Smart Object into your Street Scene Comp file.

4 Select the Move tool (⊕) and click and drag the **street.psd** image to the Street Scene Comp tab. When the Street Scene image comes forward, drag down to the image area, and then release.

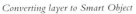

To center the placement of the layer, press and hold Shift while dragging the layer onto the destination document.

5 Press Ctrl+T (Windows) or Command+T (Mac OS) to bring up the transform bounding box. Scale the layer up by clicking and dragging any of the corners of the transform bounding box. To scale uniformly, press and hold Shift while dragging the corners of the transform box. Press Enter (Windows) or Return (Mac OS) when done.

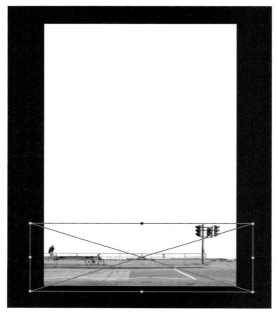

Laying the foundations.

6 Choose File > Save As to save your work. When the Save As dialog box appears make sure that you are saving the file in the native Photoshop (.PSD) format and that it is saving into the advps07lessons folder.

7 Return to the street.psd image and choose File > Close.

Adding a second image to the composition

Now you will add another image to the composition.

1 Choose File > Open and locate the **fixer upper 1.tif** file located in the advps07lessons folder.

2 Make sure the Move tool (✛) is still selected, and then click and drag the **fixer upper 1.tif** image to the tab for the Street Scene Comp. Do not release the mouse just yet. When the Street Scene Comp comes forward, drag down to the image area and then release the mouse. The **fixer upper 1.tif** image has been added as a layer to the Street Scene Comp image.

When the drag and drop technique is used the new layer is placed on top of the last active layer.

3 Double-click the name of the new layer you just placed and type **fixer upper 1**.

4 Convert the fixer upper 1 layer to a Smart Object by right-clicking the layer and selecting Convert to Smart Object.

5 In the Layers panel, drag the fixer upper 1 below the layer named straightened.

Notice that the lighting conditions are fairly similar between these two images, although the direction of the light is different.

Adding the fixer upper 1 file.

The lighting is can be easily fixed by horizontally flipping one of the images. Given that the fixer upper 1 layer has text on it, you will transform the layer named straighten instead.

6 Select the layer named straightened in the Layer's panel and press Ctrl+T (Windows) or Command+T (Mac OS).

7 Right-click the transform bounding box, and then select Flip Horizontal from the contextual menu that appears. Press Enter (Windows) or Return (Mac OS) to commit the horizontal flip.

You could also select Edit > Transform > Flip Horizontal.

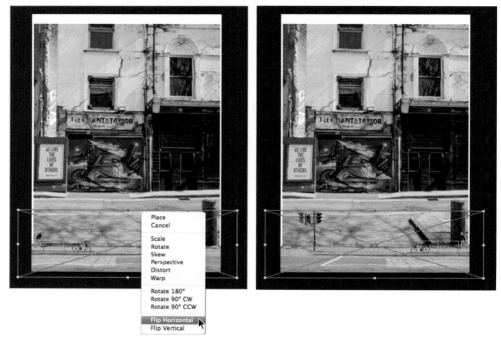

Flip the layer named straightened.   *The result.*

You will now scale down the set of buildings you added by scaling down the fixer upper 1 layer.

8 Select the fixer upper 1 layer, and press Ctrl+T (Windows) or Command+T (Mac OS) to activate the transform bounding box.

9 Press and hold Shift and drag one of the upper corners inwards to decrease the size of the layer to approximately half the size.

You can see the scale amount by looking in Width and Height in the Options bar as you drag.

10 When you are finished scaling the layer press Enter (Windows) or Return (Mac OS) to commit the transform.

11 With the Move Tool still selected, click and drag the fixer upper 1 layer so that the bottom of the buildings line up with the top of the pavement in the straightened layer.

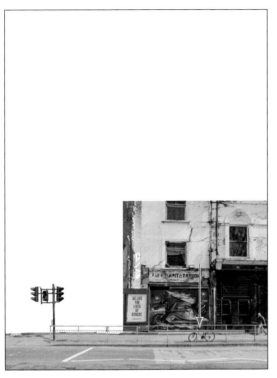

Slide the building down so that it is sitting on the street level.

Adding an image with the place feature

Now you will add a third image to the composition. Instead of dragging and dropping the image file, you will use the place feature.

1 Choose File > Place and locate and select the **fixer upper 2.tif** file in the advps07lessons folder. Click Place to place the image into your Street Scene Comp image. When you choose to place an image into an existing image it is automatically added as a Smart Object.

To help you position the layers, you will change the opacity of this layer.

2 Ensure that you have the Move tool selected and then press **5** on your keypad. This changes the opacity of the selected layer to 50%. You can also change the Opacity by using the slider in the Layers panel.

*You can press **V** to select the Move tool.*

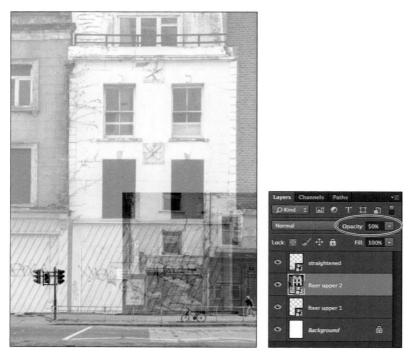

Changing the layer to 50% opacity.

Change or view the opacity in the Layers panel.

3 Press Ctrl+T (Windows) or Command+T (Mac OS); the transform bounding box appears. Click and drag the image area to move the layer up so that the base of the building sits nicely on the pavement. Don't press Enter/Return just yet.
When you activate the transform control in Photoshop control points appear to help you better control the way the transform occurs. You will use the center control point to force the transform to scale down to the pavement area.

4 Using your cursor, click and drag the central control point (⊕), (located in the center of the image) to the intersection of the pavement and the building.

5 Press and hold the Alt+Shift (Windows) or Option+Shift (Mac OS), and then drag one of the upper corners down to decrease the scale of the layer. Notice that the scale is controlled by the placement of the central control point. Press Enter (Windows) or Return (Mac OS) when you have reached a scale size of about 40%.

6 Set the opacity of the layer back to 100% by entering **100** into the Opacity text field in the Layers panel, or by pressing **0** (zero).

7 Choose File > Save.

Click and drag to scale the buildings.   *The result.*

Masking a layer

You will now begin to blend the layers together.

1 To make the join between the buildings more convincing add a layer mask to fixer upper 2 by selecting the Add layer mask icon (▣) at the bottom of the Layers panel.

2 Select the Brush tool by pressing **B**, and then Right+click (Windows) or Ctrl+click (Mac OS) on the image area to open the Brush contextual menu. Scroll down through the brushes until you see Chalk 11 px., a brush that produces a slightly broken edge.

Select the Chalk 11 px. brush.

You'll start by painting with a large Paintbrush to show what's behind the layers, and then paint back in details with a smaller sized brush.

3   Select the Layer Mask thumbnail to the right of the fixer upper 2 layer. If black is not your foreground color, press **X** to toggle your foreground and background colors.

4   Press the] key (right bracket) approximately 13 times to increase the brush size to about 100 pixels.

5   Now paint along the vertical edge of the building. Don't worry about painting away too much; masks only hide the image where you are painting black, so your image won't be deleted.

Broad brush strokes are used to paint on the mask.

6   Press **X** to switch the foreground color to white.

7   Press the [key (left bracket) approximately 5 times to reduce the size of the brush to about 50 pixels.

8   Using the Brush tool, paint the layer back in to create a nice join down the building and around the sign.

If you want to paint a straight line quickly, press the Shift key+click from one point to another using the Brush tool.

Smaller brush strokes are used to paint back detail.

The Adaptive Wide Angle filter

In this part of the lesson, you will learn to remove lens distortion in an image. You might have noticed that the adjoining edge is at a bit of a strange angle. This is a good opportunity to use one of the more advanced tools in Photoshop to fix the angle.

1   Right-click (Windows) or Ctrl+click (Mac OS) fixer upper 1 and select Edit Contents from the context menu. If a warning message appears, click OK.

2   The image opens as **fixer upper 1.psb**. You will now edit this image.

3   Choose Filter > Adaptive Wide Angle.

4 While pressing and holding the Shift key, click near the top left edge of the building and drag a line down the edge, and then release the mouse. The filter takes that line you've just created and distorts the image to follow your line.

You can continue pulling lines down using the Shift key but make sure that you do not go outside the image area. You will know if you have extended beyond the confines of the image if your purple line changes from a solid line to a dashed line. Don't click OK just yet.

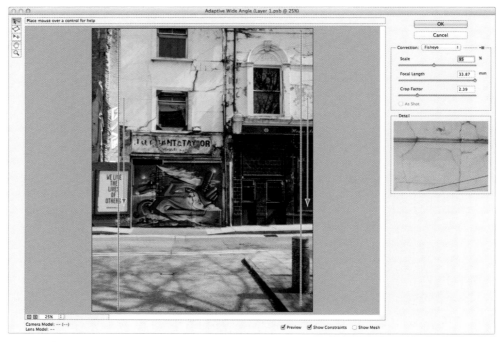

Distorting the image using the Adaptive Wide Angle filter.

5 Repeat the process using horizontal lines across the middle of the image.

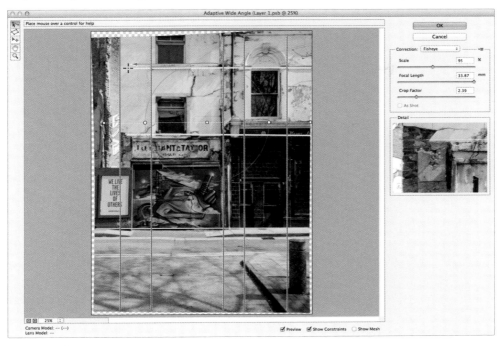

Straightening the image.

6 Click OK, choose File > Save, and then File > Close.

Using the Clone Stamp tool to copy a window

You will now use the Clone Stamp tool to copy a window from one location to another.

1 Return to your street comp image and notice that the fixer upper 1 Smart Object has updated itself.

2 Press and hold the Alt (Windows) or Option (Mac OS) key, and then select the Create a new layer button (◼) at the bottom of the Layers panel. The New Layer dialog box appears.

3 In the Name text field, type **top window**, and then click OK.

4 Select the Clone Stamp brush (▲).

5 From the Brush Preset Picker in the Options bar, choose the Chalk 11px brush.

6 Adjust the slider on the Brush Preset Picker to increase the brush to 100 pixels.

7 Click the fixer upper 1 layer and Alt+click (Windows) or Option+click (Mac OS) the inside top left corner of the lower window main pane.

Alt/Option+click the upper-left of the window to define the clone origin.

8 Click the new top window layer in the Layers panel and move the cursor to the corresponding area of the upper window pane, and then start painting. Keep painting upwards until you start to see another window frame appear Paint to the right until you start painting in the pipes on the join between the two buildings.

9 Create a new mask on the top window layer by clicking the Add layer mask icon (▣).

10 Make sure that the Brush tool is selected and then Right-click (Windows) or Ctrl+click (Mac OS) to select Soft Round Brush from the contextual menu that appears. Using the soft brush, paint along the bottom edge of the layer to blend it into the one below.

A quick extension.

Adding an additional building

You will now add a church to the image.

1 Choose File > Open and locate the **church 1.psd** file located in the advps07lessons folder. Notice there are two layers: one is the original, and the other has been straightened using the Adaptive Wide Angle filter.

2 Make sure the Move tool (✣) is still selected, and then click and drag the straightened layer to the tab for the Street Scene Comp. Do not release the mouse just yet. When the Street Scene Comp comes forward, drag down to the image area and then release the mouse. The **church 1.psd** image has been added to the Street Scene Comp image as a new layer.

3 Return to the **church 1.psd** file and choose File > Close.

4 Return to the Street Scene Comp image, double-click the new layer's name and type **church straightened**.

5 Convert the church straightened layer to a Smart Object by right-clicking (Windows) or Ctrl+clicking (Mac OS) the layer and selecting Convert to Smart Object.

6 With the church layer straightened, press Ctrl+Shift+right bracket (Windows) or Command+Shift+right bracket (Mac OS) to move the church straightened layer to the top of the layer stack.

7 Press **5** to change the opacity of the layer to 50%.

8 Press Ctrl+T (Windows) or Command+T (Mac OS) to bring up the transform bounding box and visually scale the layer down in size so that it sits nicely on top of the two buildings at the right side of the image. In this example the image was scaled down to approximately 48%. Once in place, press Return.

9 Press **0** to bring the layer back to 100% opacity.

A subtle decorative feature has been added to the image.

Blending the church

You will now create and paint on the mask of the church.

1 Create a new mask on the church layer by clicking the Add layer mask button (▣) at the bottom of the Layers panel.

2 Press **D** to select your default colors in the color picker.

3 Paint out parts of the church straightened layer to create a convincing blend. Start at the bottom, removing railings, bicycle, people, and work your way up. Take your time with this. Since you are using masks, you can easily switch from hiding the layer parts (painting with black) to revealing the layer parts (painting with white).

Blending in the church layer.

Removing some of the architecture

Once there's a nice blend, you will need to address the issue of missing architecture at the top of the church. You have two options for solving this problem: one is to recreate some of the architecture, and the other is to remove some of the architecture. In this lesson, you will remove some of the architecture. Your first task will be to remove the portion of stained-glass window that's on the left, along with a bit of the arch.

1 Select the Brush tool (✓), and then right-click the image to show the brush context menu. Scroll down in the menu and select the Chalk 11px.

2 Verify that you have the church layer mask selected and then start painting with a 45-pixel brush. You can then press the [(left bracket) several times to create a smaller brush for details.

Removing the window.

Next, you will clean up the top edge by removing the top-most decoration. When removing large spans of an image, such as this decoration, it is recommended that you Shift+Click with the Brush tool to automatically connect one point to another.

3 Go to the Brush preset picker in the Options bar and change the pixel size of the brush to **20**.

4 Focusing on the left side of the church top, click one end of the decorative top strip, and then press and hold the Shift key and click the other end of the decorative top strip.

5 Keeping the Shift key pressed, click the point where the roof steps back to meet the right side and then click the right end of the right side. You now have a stretched out 'z' shape in your mask. You will now use your lasso tool to make a selection.

6 Press the **L** key to select your Lasso tool. Press and hold the Shift key, and press the **L** key again to select the polygonal lasso tool.

7 Move your cursor to the left end of the mask line you just created, and click. Move the cursor along to the first point of your 'z' cut and click again. Repeat this along the full length of the mask cut and then up and around the top section of the church roof, until you get to the start point of the selection. When cursor shows a close circle ($\searrow_o$) you can click to close the selection.

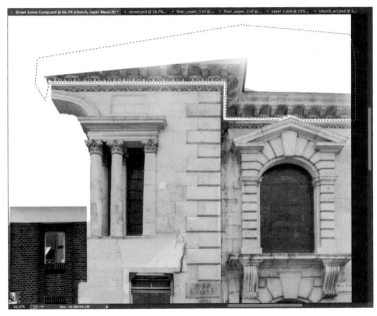

Taking the roof off the church.

8 Verify that the foreground color is still black, and then press Alt+Delete (Windows) or Option+Backspace (Mac OS) to fill this selected area with black in the mask.

9 Press Ctrl+D (Windows) or Command+D (Mac OS) to deactivate your selection.

Blending the church using Adjustment Layers

You will now tone-match the church layer, since it is much redder than the layers below.

1 Create a new curves adjustment layer on top of the church by choosing Layer > New Adjustment Layer > Curves. In the New Layer dialog box, click OK.

2 Press and hold the Alt key (Windows) or Option key (Mac OS) and click the line separating the layers between the Curves 1 layer and the church straightened layer when you see the clipping mask symbol (↓□) This links the adjustment layer to the church straightened layer so the changes yo make so not affect the layers beneath.

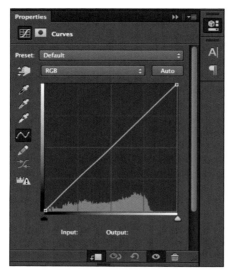

Add a new Curves adjustment layer.

3 Click the diagonal line about two-thirds of the way up and drag it slightly up. This lightens or lifts the tone of the layer.

4   Click the same line about one-third of the way up and drag it down a fraction. This effectively reduces the amount of lighter tone available in the darker parts of the layer and gives a more contrasting look.

5   Click the RGB drop-down menu and select the Red channel.

6   Click the line about half way down and drag it down slightly. This reduces the amount of red available in the combined RGB output of the layer, making the layer appear more neutral, albeit a bit yellow.

7   Click the drop-down menu again and select the Blue channel.

8   Again, click the line about halfway along and drag it up slightly.

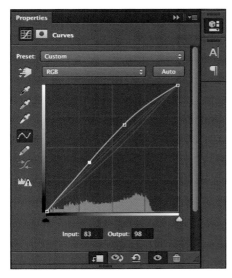

Post-color adjustments.

Final flourish

Now you will add some texture and create an overall mood grading using Color Lookup Tables.

1   Navigate to the advps07lessons folder and open **coffee stain.tif**. Using the same technique as before, drag the image onto the tab of the Street Scene Comp file and drop it onto the image.

New layer automatically linking to another.

2   Once you have placed the new layer return to the coffee stain.tif file and choose File > Close.

Notice that the new layer was automatically linked to church straightened layer. This is because a linked layer was selected when the new image layer was added. To unlink the new layer, press and hold the Alt/Option key and place the cursor between layer 1 and curves 1 in the layer stack. When you see the unclip icon (⦻) click.

3   Return to your Street Scene Comp image file and rename the layer **coffee stain**.

4   In the Layers panel choose Hard Light from the blending mode drop-down menu. This blending mode adds a distressed/retro look to the image.

5   Press **5** to reduce the opacity of the coffee stain layer down to 50% to provide a nicely muted grade while retaining the distressed look.

Top-level texture applied.

Using a color look-up table

The image now needs a final touch to give add more contrast. For this part of the lesson, you will use the Color Lookup adjustment. This flexible tool offers a number of presets to give your image a different look and feel.

1   Click the New fill or adjustment layer at the bottom of the Layers panel and select Color Lookup. The Color Lookup Properties window appears and adds an adjustment layer.

2   Click the Load 3DLUTFile drop-down menu to bring up a list of options or 'looks'. For this exercise, select filmstock_50.3dl.

3   Press the **V** key and then press the **8** key to drop the adjustment layer down to 80% to bring back some of the detail and movement in the coffee stain layer below.

Final image.

Self study

Now that you have completed this composition, experiment with some of the tools used in this exercise.

1   Create a new document and open **church 1.psd** and **fixer upper 1.tif**.

2   Using the Adaptive Wide Angle filter, straighten out the original shot.

3   Using Smart Objects and masks, add some of the windows from fixer upper 1 onto the church.

4   Experiment with the Color Lookup adjustment to give your image different looks.

Review

Questions

1   What are the benefits of using Smart Objects?

2   Why would you use masks rather than the eraser tool?

3   How would you add a warmer tone to an image using curve adjustments?

Answers

1   The benefits of using Smart Objects can be summed up in one word: flexibility. Since the Smart Object is an instanced version of an image, you can scale, filter, update, or modify the Smart Object without changing the original file and without losing any of the resolution detail or quality.

2   Once you have a mask on a layer, you can easily paint to reveal or hide parts of the layer by switching between black and white in your color picker. As long as the mask exists, your options are endless.

3   To create a warmer tone to an image using curves, you would decrease the blue curve slightly (to introduce more yellow) and increase the red curve slightly (to introduce more red). This combination of colors effectively adds more orange to the image.

Lesson 8

What you'll learn in this lesson:

- Using Oil Paint
- Using the Camera Raw filter
- Adding layer effects
- Adding lighting effects
- Adding text effects

Creating Special Effects

Photoshop is known for its ability to create special effects. In this lesson, you'll learn about several non-destructive effects that you can apply to your images. You will also have an opportunity to explore advanced effects that you can apply on your own.

Starting up

In this lesson, you will start with a Photoshop file that has already been layered and masked using the steps covered in previous lessons. Make sure that you have loaded the advpslessons folder onto your hard drive from the supplied DVD. For more detailed instructions, see "Loading lesson files" in the Starting up section of this book.

See Lesson 8 in action!

Use the accompanying video to gain a better understanding of how to use some of the features shown in this lesson. You can find the video tutorial for this lesson on the included DVD.

Using Oil Paint as a Smart Filter

In this first section you will take advantage of Smart filters to create a painterly effect on your image. You can use Oil Paint as a Smart Filter to non-destructively add a classic, hand-painted look to an image. The filter works well with medium to high-resolution RGB images. You will work with a 1500 × 1139 pixel image at 300 ppi.

1   Choose File > Browse in Bridge to open Adobe Bridge.

2   Navigate to the advps08lessons folder contained within the advpslessons folder on your computer, and double-click **advps0801.psd** to open it. If an embedded Profile Mismatch dialog box appears, leave it at the defaults and click OK.

3   Choose File > Save As. In the Save As dialog box, type **advps0801_work.psd** in the File Name text field. Make sure it is in the Photoshop (PSD) format and that you are saving the file into the advps08lessons folder. If a dialog box about Maximize Compatibility appears, leave the option on and click OK, and then click Save.

4   If the Layers panel is not visible, choose Window > Layers, then select the Lagoon layer.

5   Choose Filter > Convert for Smart Filters. If an Adobe Photoshop warning dialog box appears, click OK.

6   Choose Filter > Oil Paint. The Oil Paint dialog box appears. Keep this dialog box open for the next part of the lesson.

Oil Paint Filter applied to the Lagoon layer using the default settings.

The Oil Paint filter requires RGB images and a supported graphics card. If it does not work as expected, it could mean that your graphics card driver is out-of-date. You can find a list of video cards tested by Adobe by visiting adobe.com *and searching for "Photoshop tested video cards."*

Exploring Oil Paint options

In this next part of the lesson, you have an opportunity to review the Oil Paint options.

As you work in this section, you might need to zoom in to see the stroke details. When zoomed in, you can press and hold the Spacebar and click and drag to pan the image.

1   Experiment with the Stylization control by moving the slider to the right to create longer strokes and to the left to create shorter strokes. For this part of the lesson, you can choose any size. In this example **1.78** is used.

2   Experiment with the Cleanliness control by moving the slider to the left to add more detail and texture to the brush strokes. Moving to the right uses less detail and looser strokes. In this example a value of **1** is used.

3   Scale controls the size of the brush strokes. Our example uses a value of **1.93**. You can experiment and use any value you want.

4   The Bristle Detail controls bristle details from less (left) to more (right). This interacts with other settings, so you might need to adjust other settings, such as Stylization and so on. If you don't see any effects, zoom in closer or try moving the other settings toward the middle. Our example uses a value of **7.1**.

5   Angular Direction is the angle of light source (from above) and can have a very dramatic effect, especially on water. Our example uses a value of **90**. You can set your Angular Direction to 90, or pick a value that you prefer.

6 Shine controls the contrast and depth of the paint; left is less depth and right is more. Our example uses a value of **2.15**. Again, you can pick a different value. When you are satisfied with your settings in the Oil Paint filter, click OK.

You can reset all settings by pressing and holding the Alt key (Windows) or Option key (Mac OS) to change the Cancel button to a Reset button, then click Reset. The reset hot key works with many menus throughout Photoshop. Some menus might remember your last settings.

Explore the special effect settings for the Oil Paint filter, including Shine to add depth.

The power of Smart Filters

When you use the Smart Filter feature on a layer, you essentially embed the original image data into your Photoshop file. This allows you the opportunity to make changes throughout your image editing process without destroying original image data.

1   Toggle the Oil Paint filter on/off by clicking the visibility icon (👁) next to Smart Filters in the Layers panel, to see a before/after effect.

Leave the filter visibility for your Oil Paint filter turned on.

Toggle the visibility of the Oil Paint filter.

2   Double-click the words Oil Paint in the Layers panel. You now see the same settings you used and can make any adjustments that you might need or want to make. Click OK.

3   Choose File > Save.

Some Photoshop features might not be available when using Smart Filters. For example, you cannot use the Brush tool on the Lagoon layer; to use this tool, you first need to rasterize the layer. You can either double-click the Smart Filter icon in the lower-right corner of the Layer Thumbnail to open the original image and apply your effect, or you can right-click (Windows) or Ctrl+click (Mac OS) the layer and select Rasterize layer.

Deleting a Smart Filter

If you don't want a Smart Filter, you can drag it to the trash can icon (🗑) in the Layers panel. To see how this works, you will delete the Smart Filter, and bring it right back with the Undo feature.

1   Drag the Oil Paint Smart Filter to the Trash can (🗑) at the bottom of the Layers panel to delete the Smart Filter effect.

2   Choose Edit > Step Backward to restore the Oil Paint Smart Filter effect.

Using Camera Raw as a Smart Filter

Camera Raw refers to a proprietary feature for professional cameras known as "shooting raw" image data, as well as a feature in Photoshop. In other words, you can configure certain cameras so that whatever light passes through the lens/filters is captured in its raw format, then use Adobe's Camera Raw filter to further process the image. This avoids artifacts caused by JPEG compression, and can make a big difference in the quality of the image. It can also result in big file sizes.

Some cameras can shoot both Raw and JPEG data directly, even while tethered to a laptop with Lightroom. Recent improvements to high-end digital cameras have reduced the need to shoot raw images. Raw files typically have filename extensions of .crw or .cr2 (for Canon cameras) or .nef (for Nikon Electronic Format). You do not need raw images to use the Camera Raw filter.

1   Turn on the top Parrots layer by clicking the visibility icon (👁) next to the thumbnail of the parrots in the Layers panel.

This layer has already been masked using the steps covered in Lesson 3, "Advanced Selection Techniques."

2   Click the word Parrots in the Layers panel to select the Parrots layer.

Where you click in the layers panel can make a BIG difference. For example, a common pitfall is mistakenly clicking the mask icon (which would target the mask) that provides entirely different results.

3   Choose Filter > Convert for Smart Filters.

If a dialog box about Smart Filters appears, click OK. You can click the Don't show again check box, and then click OK to make the dialog box remember your choice and not appear again.

4   Choose Filter > Camera Raw Filter, the Camera Raw dialog box appears.

5 Double-click the Zoom tool at the top of the Camera Raw dialog box to change the zoom to 100%, and then use the Hand tool to pan, or reposition the image of the parrots.

This image has already been color corrected so few adjustments are needed. However, you might want to explore some special effects, which you will do later in this lesson.

6 Click the HSL/Grayscale icon (▦) Windows or (▤) (Mac OS) and explore the possibilities for changing the colors of the parrot's feathers using adjustments on the Hue, Saturation, and Luminance panels. There are no set values that you must change in this step but keep in mind the following as you make changes:

Hue: Changes the color.

Saturation: Changes the brightness of a color. For instance a desaturated parrot would appear as a grayscale image.

Luminance: Changes the lightness of an image. When you bring down the luminance you fade the image.

You can also double-click any slider in the Camera Raw filter to reset it back to the default setting.

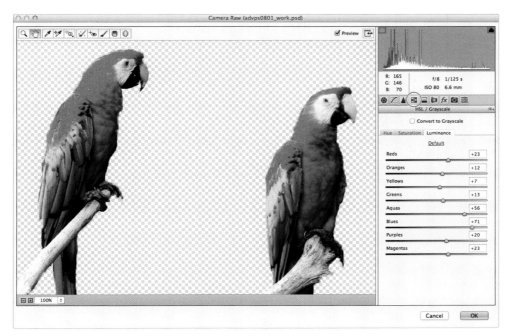

Explore the possibilities using the Camera Raw filter for HSL/Grayscale to enhance colors of the parrot's feathers. You can use any settings you want.

7 When you are done experimenting, click OK and choose File > Save to save your file.

Since this is a Smart Filter, you can always come back to make additional adjustments by double-clicking the Camera Raw filter in the Layers panel.

Using the Mask in the Smart Object

Notice that the mask for the Parrots layer no longer appears in the Layers panel. However, since you converted this layer for Smart Filters, you can still access the original mask.

1   Double-click the thumbnail of the Parrots in the Layers panel. If you see a dialog box about editing the contents, click OK.

You are now in a the embedded file called **Parrots.psb**. This is similar to a linked file that you can edit and update.

2   Select the Channels panel. If you do not see the Channels panel, choose Window > Channels.

3   Select the visibility icon (👁) to the left of the thumbnail for the Parrots Mask, then select the words "Parrots Mask" to display and select the mask. When a mask is selected a default color of light red appears. This represents the area that is masked. Notice that the bottom of the image and a few other areas are not completely masked and do not display as light red, these areas are not masked.

Click the Parrots Mask channel to show the masked area.

4   Select the Brush tool in the Tools panel and paint over the areas that are not light red. When you paint with black you are painting masking material if you press **X** to switch to white you are erasing the mask material.

If necessary, reset the Brush tool by right-clicking (Windows) or Ctrl+clicking (Mac OS) its icon at the top of screen in the Tool options bar and choosing Reset tool. Since the bottoms of the branches are cropped out, you do not need to work on that area.

You can change the brush size by pressing the bracket [ ] keys and paint in the appropriate areas to adjust the mask. Pressing the X key will toggle between adding and removing the mask.

5   Click the Close box next to the filename **Parrots.psb**, and then click Save to update the mask. If needed, click the Layers panel tab to show it instead of the Channels panel.

Adding Layer Style effects

Layer Styles are one of the most powerful features for Photoshop. For example, you can change the colors of the parrots to any other colors.

1   Select the Parrots layer in the Layers panel, and then select the visibility icon (👁) next to the corresponding Camera Raw Filter to turn it off.

The Camera Raw Filter will interact and interfere with what we are about to do; you can turn it back on later.

2   Click the Add a layer style button (🖹) at the bottom of the Layers panel, then select Gradient Overlay. The Layer Style dialog box appears with the settings for Gradient Overlay visible.

You can use the settings in this example or experiment on your own.

3   Change the Blend Mode to Hue.

4   Type **89** into the Opacity text field.

5 From the Gradient preset drop-down menu choose Transparent Rainbow.
Note that you can create your own gradient by double-clicking the present gradient.
This opens a Gradient editor that allows you to edit existing gradients and make new
ones of your own.

Changing the setting of the Gradient Overlay.

You can create custom gradients by double-clicking the gradient.

6 Leave the Style set to Linear and type **105** into the Angle text field, and then type
96 into the Scale text field.

Note that you can click and drag directly in the image area to reposition the gradient.

7 Click OK when you are satisfied with your gradient, then toggle the visibility for both
the Gradient Overlay and/or the Camera Raw filter. Leave the visibility turned on.

8 Choose File > Save.

*Get in the habit of selecting styles by selecting the style names. Selecting the check boxes activates
the style, but does not show the style's options.*

Adding lighting effects

Lighting is everything in photography. The word *photograph* stems from the Greek words
photos, meaning light and *graphos*, meaning writing. In other words, photography means
writing with light or perhaps painting with light. Without light, there can be no image.

For best results, you will need to take control of lighting the subject with professional
equipment. For example, professional photographers use a variety of strobe lights, gels,
flashguns, light boxes, umbrellas, etc., against an assortment of backdrops. Visit the site
http://www.lightingdiagrams.com/ for excellent resources, including a free online lighting
diagram creator, and to collaborate with other photographers to share ideas.

If you are not a professional photographer, you could hire one or search for some stock photography from sites such as *iStockphoto.com*, which is what we did for these lesson files. Regardless of the source of your images, which is frequently from mobile phones, you can add amazing lighting effects using Photoshop.

Adding interesting lighting effects

In this next part of the lesson, you will add interesting lighting effects to the Flowers layer.

1   Reveal the Flowers layer by clicking the visibility icon (👁) in the Layers panel next to the thumbnail of the flowers, and then click the word Flowers to select the layer.

2   Choose Filter > Convert for Smart Filters. If a dialog box about filters appears, click OK.

3   Choose Filter > Render > Lighting Effects.

Click the Presets drop-down menu in the top left area of the screen and explore each option that appears, including 2 O'Clock Spotlight, Blue Omni, etc. Notice that the settings in the Properties panel on the right change with each preset. Notice also that the various controls on the image change with each preset position.

4   Choose the Default preset when you are done experimenting so that you can create a custom light for the flowers.

5   In the Properties panel on the right, you see that Spot light is selected by default. From the drop-down menu select Point light, then Infinite, and then back to Spot to see the differences between the three lights:

- **Point**: shines light in all directions from directly above the image, such as a light bulb.

- **Infinite**: shines light across an entire plane, such as the sun.

- **Spot**: casts an elliptical beam of light. The line in the preview window defines the light direction and angle, plus the various handle controls on the image define the edges of the ellipse.

6   Position your cursor over the ellipse controls, in the preview area, and notice that the words Move, Rotate, and Scale Width appear. If you don't see Scale Width appear, position the cursor near the top or bottom handle. If you still don't see these controls choose View > Show All.

7   Position your cursor near the small white circle, and then drag to resize the width
of the ellipse. Try repositioning and rotating the light so that it looks similar to our
example.

Use the various control handles to reposition, rotate, and resize the ellipse for the spotlight.

8   Keep this file open for the next part of the lesson.

Adjusting the lighting

You can use the settings in the top half of the Properties panel to take control of lighting
a subject. For example, you can control the color of light by clicking the white swatch, as
well as adjust the intensity. This is similar to putting a filter or gel on a light and adjusting
the brightness of the bulb. You can also adjust the Hotspot (inner oval on the image) to
control the range of lighting.

You can use the settings in the lower half of the Properties panel (divided by a barely
visible line above Colorize) to adjust these options for the *entire set* of lights:

- **Colorize**: controls the tint of the overall lighting. You can click the swatch to change
  the color.

- **Exposure**: controls highlight and shadow detail.

- **Gloss**: determines how much surfaces reflect light.

- **Metallic**: determines which is more reflective: the light or the object on which the light
  is cast.

- **Ambience**: diffuses the light as if it were combined with other light in a room, such as sunlight or fluorescent light. Choose a value of 100 to use only the light source, or a value of −100 to remove the light source.

- **Texture**: applies a texture channel that lets you control lighting effects using grayscale images (called bump maps) to simulate 3D.

The Lighting Effects *filter works with 8-bit RGB images ONLY, and requires a supported video card.*

Adding sunlight effects

Now you will adjust the light of the flowers so the image looks as though light is leaking down from the forest canopy on to the flowers.

1   Increase the Spot light intensity to about **42** in the Properties panel and enlarge the Hotspot to around **90** by dragging the sliders.

2   Adjust the ellipse dimensions by dragging the appropriate adjustment handles, and then zooming in to 100% using the shortcut menu in the lower left corner of the screen.

  Although there are no tools available, you can pan around by dragging the scroll bars alongside the artwork area, or by pressing and holding the spacebar while dragging.

3   Experiment with Exposure, Gloss, and any other settings to create an interesting effect. No specific settings are required. In this example an exposure value of **–6** was used. A Gloss of **–11**, Metallic of **–2** and Ambience of **11** were also set.

Adjust the Lighting Effects properties to gain the desired effect.

It's important not to overexpose the image or create unrealistic shadows if you want the image to look realistic and convincing. On the other hand, you might want to go for a more surrealistic or amusing effect.

4   Toggle the Preview option off/on at the top of the screen (to see a before/after effect), make any additional adjustments, and then click OK when you are ready.

Creating a Depth of Field effect

You can create depth of field illusions by moving images to the foreground (top) layer. The keys to success are good quality images, good masking, and convincing lighting.

Right now, the flowers are behind the parrots and they are in a shaded area, so it doesn't look very convincing. You will now change that with a few strategic moves.

1   Double-click the Hand tool (✍) in the Tools panel to fit the image in the window.

2   Select the Move tool (✛) and activate Auto-Select in the Options bar at the top of the screen. Now use the Move tool to drag the flowers behind the parrots.

The Auto-Select option works well when transparency isn't used; trying to click a transparent image might result in selecting lower layers. If this happens to you, turn off the option and select the layer in the Layers panel. You can also press and hold the Ctrl/Command key to turn on Auto-Select only when you want to use it.

3   In the Layers panel, drag the Flowers layer to the top of the panel above the Parrots layer. The flowers are now in front of the parrots. Position the flowers to the left (where it's lighter) to make the depth of field effect more convincing. Zoom in to find a good place for the flowers in front of the parrot or branch.

You can also position the parrots wherever you want; for example, the parrot on the left could be looking at the flowers. Since everything is a live effect using Smart Filters, you can double-click to tweak the elements that want, including the masks.

4 Choose File > Save to save your finished version.

You can zoom in and out by pressing and holding the Alt key (Windows) or Option key (Mac OS) and rolling the scroll wheel on your mouse.

The composition of the birds.

Adding text effects

In this next part of the lesson, you will add some interesting text effects.

1 Double-click the Hand tool in the Tools panel to fit the image in the window.

2 Click the word Flowers in the Layers panel to select the Flowers layer and ensure that the new text layer is created above the layer.

3 Click the Text tool in the Tools panel, and then click in the cloudy area between the palm trees. In the Options bar choose the font Adobe Caslon Bold Italic with a size of **42**, and then type **Parrot Paradise**.

4 Move your mouse below the text until you see the Move tool appear, and then position the text at the top of the image as shown below. Note that you do not need to switch to the Move tool in the Tools panel. You can also press and hold the Ctrl/Command key to switch temporarily to the Move tool.

5 Select the text and then click the color swatch in the Text tool Options bar. Click any color in the image area to apply it to your selected text. This example uses a color sampled from the parrot on the left. Click OK to close the Color Picker when you find a color you like.

You can apply a color from your image to your text.

6 Click the Create Warped Text icon (⬛) in the Text tool options bar. The Warp Text dialog box appears.

7 Experiment with each of the Warp Text styles. Be sure to slide each of the options to discover the possibilities. This example uses the **Flag Style** with a Horizontal Bend of **+42** and **0** for Horizontal and Vertical Distortion.

8 Click OK in the Warp Text dialog box, and then click the checkmark icon in the Text tool Options bar to commit the changes.

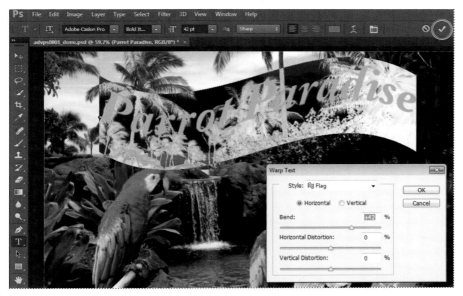

This example uses the Warp Option Flag Style with a Horizontal Bend of 42; you can use any warp options you want.

Adding Swash Characters

Some OpenType fonts, such as Adobe Caslon Bold Italic (included with Creative Cloud) have special Swash characters that can add appealing special effects to text. Note that very few fonts have this particular option and it is only available in the italic cut.

1 Use the Text tool to select the words *Parrot Paradise*.

2 If the Character panel is not visible, choose Window > Character, then select OpenType > Swash from the Character panel menu.

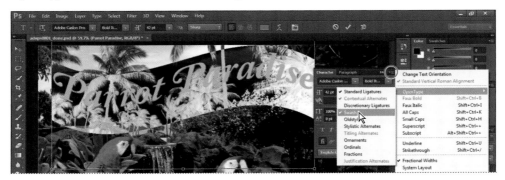

You can access special characters such as Swash from the Character panel menu OpenType options.

3 Click the checkmark icon in the Text tool Options bar to commit the changes.

Self study

In this lesson, you were introduced to several special effects. On your own, add a few more Layer Styles to the Parrot Paradise text, such as Bevel & Emboss and an Outer Glow effect, using the *fx* button at the bottom of the Layers panel as shown. Also experiment with additional Smart Filters by applying some effects to your other layers.

Add a Bevel & Emboss plus an Outer Glow effect to the text.

Review

Questions

1 What is the main advantage of using Smart Filters?

2 Which special effect allows you to simulate sunlight? Where can you find the feature?

3 How can you edit the settings for a Smart Filter?

Answers

1 The main advantage of using a Smart Filter is that they are non-destructive to the original image and you can make edits to your filter at a later time.

2 To simulate sunlight, use the Lighting Effects filter found under Filter > Render > Lighting Effects.

3 You can edit the settings for a Smart Filter by double-clicking the name of the filter in the Layers panel.

What you'll learn in this lesson:

- Using shapes in Photoshop
- Importing vector graphics
- Saving custom shapes
- Using type as vector shapes
- Masking with vector shapes

Advanced Use of the Vector Tools

In this lesson, you'll take your knowledge of vector tools further by building custom shapes and masks, and by applying type effects in Photoshop.

Starting up

Before starting, make sure that your tools and panels are consistent by resetting your preferences. See "Resetting Adobe Photoshop CC preferences" in the Starting up section of this book. You will work with several files from the advps09lessons folder in this lesson. Make sure that you have loaded the advpslessons folder onto your hard drive from the supplied DVD. See "Loading lesson files" in the Starting up section of this book.

See Lesson 9 in action!

Use the accompanying video to gain a better understanding of how to use some of the features shown in this lesson. You can find the video tutorial for this lesson on the included DVD.

Taking advantage of vector objects in Photoshop CC

By taking advantage of the vector tools in Photoshop, you can create scalable artwork that is useful for print, web, and application development. Vector graphics are mathematically created so you can scale them without degradation or pixelization in the image.

You probably use Adobe Illustrator for vector graphics, since it is predominantly a vector-creation application. Even though there are vector capabilities in Photoshop CC, you should continue creating most of your vector graphics in Illustrator. The vector capabilities in Photoshop help in other creative ways, such as creating vector masks or adding vector shapes for special effects. By creating vector images in Photoshop, you also open up opportunities to integrate vector shapes with your image.

Location of the vector tools

The vector tools in Photoshop are all located in the third (lower) section of your Tools panel.

In this section you'll find the Pen tool for creating custom paths, the Type tool, the Path Selection tool for selecting your paths, and the Shape tools. Keep in mind that each of these tools has additional hidden tools that you can access by clicking and holding the tool.

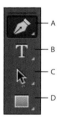

A. Pen tool. B. Type tool.
C. Path Selection tool. D. Shape tools.

Opening the image

In this lesson, you'll start with a beach image and finish with a postcard that includes vector masks, text, and shapes.

1   Choose File > Open and navigate to the advps09lessons folder. Locate and open the file named **advps0901.psd**. An image of a sand snowman appears.

2   Choose File > Save As. In the Save As dialog box, type **advps0901_work** into the Name text field; make sure the format stays as Photoshop (PSD) and that you are saving into the advps09lessons folder. Click Save.

Starting with a vector shape

In this part of the lesson, you'll create a simple rectangle. You'll then integrate it into the image using Photoshop tools, such as masks and blending modes.

1   With the **advps0901_work** file still open, select the Rectangle tool from the Vector tools section of the tools panel (directly above Hand tool).

2   If you cannot see your entire image, press Ctrl+0 (zero) (Windows) or Command+0 (Mac OS).

3   Choose View > New Guide. In the New Guide panel choose Vertical, and then type **50%** into the Position text field.

4   With the Rectangle tool click and drag from about the 50% mark to the right side of your image.

Click and drag with the Rectangle Shape tool.

When you release your mouse, you'll see that an additional layer has been added to your Layers panel, and you'll also see the Properties panel. The Properties panel allows you to apply a fill and stroke to your shape and make adjustments to the stroke style. In this example, you'll just change the Fill.

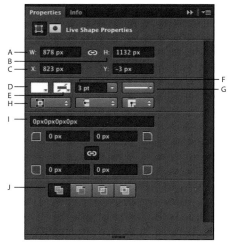

A new shape layer is added.

The Properties panel.
A. Width. B. Height. C. X,Y Coordinates. D. Fill.
E. Stroke. F. Stroke size. G. Stroke Options.
H. Set stroke alignment, cap height, and corners.
I. Rounded corner radius. J. Pathfinder options.

5   In the Properties panel, click the Set shape fill type and select White from the Swatches that appear.

Select white for the fill.

6   Click the Mask icon to show the masking options for your shape.

7   Click and drag the Feather slider towards the right to see how you can soften the edge of a vector shape. Drag the slider back to the left to see that this change is dynamic. Notice that you can make these changes repeatedly without losing the original vector shape.

8   Set the Feather to about **50 px**.

Feather the vector shape using the Properties panel.

Adding a mask

You will now add a mask to this layer to fade the shape into the image.

1   In the Layers panel, click the Add layer mask button. A mask is added to the right of the Rectangle 1 shape layer.

2   Press **D** to make sure that you are back to the default foreground and background colors. When the mask is selected, white is the foreground color.

3 Select the Gradient tool from the Tools panel; then, click and Shift+drag the cursor from the right side of the shape to the left side. Note that in this example, the gradient started a little bit in from the side on the right. You can recreate this gradient over and over again without undoing the step, since the mask overwrites itself each time. Note that you have created the gradient on the mask, not on the actual shape.

Pressing and holding the Shift key constrains the gradient to a straight path.

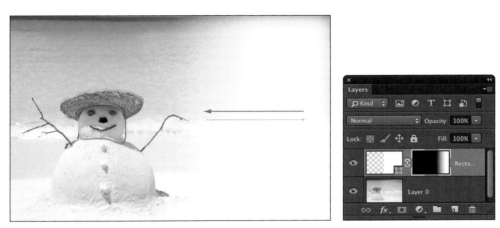

Click and drag the gradient from the right side of the rectangle shape to the left.   *The gradient is added to the mask.*

You will now turn off the visibility of this shape layer so you can focus on the text that you'll add to this image.

4 Click the visibility eye icon to the left of the Rectangle 1 layer.

5 Choose File > Save. Keep the file open for the next part of the lesson.

Adding vector text

Text that you create in Photoshop is vector type, and depending upon how you save the file, it will remain in the vector state. The following formats will keep your text as vector when saved:

- Photoshop
- EPS
- PDF

If you choose to save in another format (for example, TIF), your vector text will rasterize. To rasterize means that the vector data, such as vector shapes and text, convert to pixels. The resolution of your rasterized text depends on the resolution of the image.

A vector image is mathematically created and is scalable. The rasterized text is pixelated and cannot scale successfully.

1   With the **advps0901_work** file still open, select the background layer in the Layers panel, and then select the Type tool (T). The available options change in the Options bar at the top.

2   From the Set the font family drop-down menu, choose the font family that you have available in a bold font style. For this example, Myriad Pro was selected.

3   Change the font style to Bold, and then enter **90** into the Font size text field. Make sure that the Left align text icon (▤) is selected.

Select a font family that has a bold style and change the size to 90.

4   Click the Toggle Character (▤) to open the Character and Paragraph panel. Change the Leading (space between the lines of text) to **65 pt**.

5   Click the Color box and then click in the dark blue at the top of the image to sample that color, and then click OK.

If you like, sample a color directly in your Color Picker window.

Open the Character panel and change the leading to 65 pt.

6   Click and drag starting from about the halfway point in the image to the right edge to create a text area.

Create a text area.

7   Type the following, making sure to press Return after each word:

TRADE
SNOW
FOR
SAND

If you do not have room to type all the text, you can click and drag the left middle handle towards the left side of your image to expand the text area.

8 Press Ctrl+A (Windows) or Command+A (Mac OS) to select all the text.

You will now use a keyboard shortcut to adjust the tracking of the text. Tracking adjusts the space between multiple letters.

9 Press and hold the Alt (Windows) or Option (Mac OS) key, and then press the left arrow (left arrow) key to decrease the spacing in between all the letters. You can do this to any amount that you want. In this example, Alt/Option+left arrow was pressed three times.

Decrease the space in between the letters.

10 When you are finished editing your text, press Ctrl+Enter (Windows) or Command+Return (Mac OS) to commit your changes. You can also click the Commit check box (✓) located on the right side of the Options panel.

11 If necessary, select the Move tool to reposition the text area so it is centered vertically on the right side of your image.

12 Choose File > Save. Keep this file open for the next part of the lesson.

Converting your text to a path

In many cases, you might need to send your artwork to someone who might not have the font family you used installed on their computer. In these cases, you can convert your text to paths in Photoshop.

1   Select the Move tool (⊹) from the Tools panel and make sure that you still have your Type layer selected in the Layer's panel.

2   From the Type menu, select Convert to Shape. Your type layer is now a shape layer. You can test this by using your vector selection tools.

3   To see that you have converted your text into vector shapes, select the Path Selection tool from the Tools panel and click the text. You can see that the text is no longer live text but it is created from vector paths.

Convert the text into vector shapes.

You will now change the way this text interacts with the underlying image by changing the blending mode.

4   Select the text layer in the Layers panel and click and drag it above the Rectangle 1 shape layer.

5   From the Layers panel, choose Color Burn from the Set the blending mode drop-down menu. The text now interacts with the content below it.

Change the blending mode to Color Burn.   *The result.*

Adding a stroke to the text

In this next step, you'll use a layer style to add a stroke to your vector text.

1   Click the Add layer style button from the bottom of the Layers panel and select Stroke from the menu that appears; the Layer Style dialog box appears.

Add the Stroke layer style.

2 In the Layer Styles dialog box, leave the Size set to 3, but change the Position to Center. This changes the alignment of the stroke.

3 Click the Set color of stroke color box, located to the right of Color. When the Color Picker appears, click in the upper-left area to select White, and then click OK.

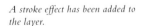

Change the position and color of the stroke.

4 Click OK in the Layer Style dialog box to see the stroke applied to your vector text.

A stroke effect has been added to the layer.   *The result.*

You can turn off and on the Stroke effect by clicking the visibility icon to the left of Stroke in the Layers panel.

Adding a drop shadow

In this next part, you'll add a drop shadow to the text and then save your combination of styles.

1   With the Trade snow layer still active, click the Add layer style button at the bottom of the Layers panel, and then select Drop Shadow. The Layer Style dialog box appears with the Drop Shadow options visible.

2   Position the Layer Style dialog box so you can also see the preview on your image. Click and drag the shadow that is applied to your image to see that you can change the distance and angle visually. You can position the shadow any way you like for this lesson.

Click and drag in the image area to visually change the distance and angle of the drop shadow.

3 Click the Set color of shadow box to the right of the Blend Mode. When the Color Picker dialog box appears, position your cursor over the darker part of the ocean (at the top of your image) and click to sample the dark blue. Click OK to set the drop shadow color.

```
Color Picker (Drop Shadow Color)
                                              OK
                            new
                                            Cancel

                                         Add to Swatches
                           current
                                         Color Libraries

                       ⦿ H: 216 °     ○ L: 41
                       ○ S: 64 %      ○ a: -4
                       ○ B: 64 %      ○ b: -43

                       ○ R: 59         C: 92 %
  ☐ Only Web Colors    ○ G: 100        M: 62 %
                       ○ B: 162        Y: 7 %
                       # 3b64a2        K: 1 %
```

Change the shadow to a sampled color of blue.

4 Slide the Size slider to the right to increase the shadow size to about 65 px.

Your shadow is not showing up in the text, which is the effect that is desired for this lesson. If you need a drop shadow through the objects on your layer, you can uncheck Layer Knocks Out Drop Shadow at the bottom of the Layer Styles dialog box.

5 Click Blending Options: Custom at the top of the list of Styles on the left side of the Layer Style dialog box.

6 Drag the Fill Opacity slider all the way to the left until it reaches 0%. By reducing the Fill to zero (0%), you essentially remove the visibility of the actual layer content and show only the effects.

Change the Fill Opacity to zero (0%).

Once you start creating combinations of styles, you can save them for future use.

7 Click New Style on the right side of the Layer Style dialog box. Leaving the settings as they are, type **My Text Style** into the text field. Click OK.

8 Click OK in the Layer Style dialog box. You will use your saved style later in this lesson.

Using a custom shape

In this part of the lesson, you'll learn about some of the other shapes that are available in Photoshop.

1   Click and hold the Rectangle tool to see other available vector shape options.

Notice that in addition to the Rectangle tool, you can select a Rounded Rectangle, Ellipse, Polygon, Line and Custom Shape. You can set the properties of these objects (such as fill, stroke and corner radius) at any time using the Options bar or the Properties panel.

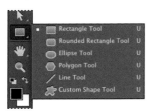

Other available shape options.

In this next part of the exercise, you'll focus on the Custom Shape tool.

2   From the Rectangle tool menu, select Custom Shape. The Options bar changes to show the Custom Shape options.

3   Click the Shape drop-down picker to see that there are a variety of custom shapes that you can choose. The shape that you are going to use is not here, but stored in a library that you will add to this list.

4   Make sure that you have the Shape drop-down menu open, and then click the gear icon on the right side. From that menu, choose Nature. When the dialog box appears asking whether you want to Replace shapes, click OK. You see new shapes added to your list.

Appending shapes keeps your current list of shapes and adds new custom shapes.

5   Select any of the snowflakes from the list of nature shapes. In this example, Snowflake 3 is used.

6   Click and drag a snowflake shape anywhere in the image. If you want to reposition it, press and hold the Ctrl (Windows) or Command (Mac OS) key to temporarily switch to the Move tool. You can also choose the Move tool from the Tools panel. Exact placement of this snowflake is not important.

Click and drag to create the shape.

Press and hold the Shift key as you drag to keep your shape proportional.

7   In the Layers panel, double-click the Shape 1 layer thumbnail you just created, and then select white from the Color Picker when it appears. Click OK.

You will now apply your saved style to the snowflake.

8 With the Snowflake 3 shape layer still selected, choose Window > Styles. From the panel menu, choose Small list to change the display of styles in the panel to a list of style names.

9 Scroll to the bottom of the list and locate your saved style. (Remember that you called it My Text Style.) Click it. The style is applied to your snowflake.

Choose your style.

The style is applied to the snowflake shape.

If you don't want to see the paths, press Ctrl+Shift+H (Windows) or Command+Shift+H (Mac OS). You can also select View > Extras > Target Path.

10 To make the snowflake shape a little less obvious, change the Opacity in the Layers panel to **20%**.

11 Choose File > Save. Keep this file open for the next part of this lesson.

Pasting vector objects from Illustrator

In this next part of the lesson, you'll take a vector object that is copied from Illustrator and turn it into a custom shape in Photoshop.

1 Launch Adobe Illustrator. If you subscribe to Adobe's Creative Cloud, you have access to Adobe Illustrator and can download it as part of your subscription.

2 From Adobe Illustrator, choose File > Open. Navigate to the advps09lessons folder and double-click the file named **advps09_footprints.ai**. Artwork for footprints appears.

3   In Adobe Illustrator, choose the Selection tool (▸), and then press Ctrl+A (Windows) or Command+A (Mac OS) to select all the artwork.

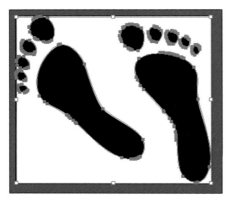

The selected Illustrator object.

4   Choose Edit > Copy, and then File > Close, do not save any changes. Return to Photoshop.

Note that you should not have any layers active when you paste a path from Illustrator. If a layer is active, you'll end up creating a mask of the active layer with your shape.

5   Make sure you have no layers active in Photoshop by selecting Select > Deselect Layers.

6   Choose Edit > Paste. A dialog box appears offering you the option to paste your vector object as a Smart Object, Pixels, Path, or Shape Layer. Choose Paths and click OK. The path of the footprint artwork appears on the image.

Choose to paste the Path.   *The path is placed on the image.*

7   Choose Edit > Define Custom Shape. When the Shape Name dialog box appears, type **Footprints**, and then click OK.

8 You don't need the active path right now because you have it stored for future use. To eliminate the footprint path, choose Window > Paths and drag the Work Path to the trash can at the bottom of the Paths panel.

Drag the Work Path to the Trash to delete the active path.

9 Choose the Custom Shape tool, and then click the Shape drop-down menu to see that your new Footprints shape has been added to the selection of shapes.

The saved shape is available as a custom shape.

10 Click and drag to create the footprint shape in the lower-left corner. Choose any size and position you want.

11 If you do not see the Styles panel, choose Window > Styles and then apply your saved My Text Style to the footprint shape.

12 Choose File > Save to save this file. Keep it open for the next part of this lesson.

Adding the Illustrator logo

In this next part of the lesson, you'll add the company logo. To keep the logo as a vector object, you will choose to Place the logo.

1 In Photoshop, choose File > Place.

2 When the Place dialog box appears, navigate to the advps09lessons folder and double-click to open the **advps09_logo.ai** artwork. Click OK when the Place PDF dialog box appears, leaving the settings at their defaults. The logo is placed and has transform handles ready for you to resize and position the logo.

3 Click and drag the logo art to the lower-right corner of the image, and then press Enter (Windows) or Return (Mac OS).

Drag the placed Illustrator artwork to the lower-right corner.

Since you placed this Illustrator artwork, it is automatically converted to a Smart Object. This means that you can resize it at any time and even continue to edit the artwork in Illustrator. In this next section, you'll reposition the SNOWBIRD text to the left of the Travels text so it fits better into the image.

4 In the Layers panel, double-click the advps09_logo layer thumbnail. A warning appears indicating that you must save the file in the same location. Click OK. You artwork is then launched in Adobe Illustrator.

If you see another warning about the artwork being modified outside Adobe Illustrator, click OK.

5   Using your Selection tool in Adobe Illustrator, click the SNOWBIRD text and drag it to the left of the Travel text. Try to align SNOWBIRD as best as you can with the Travel text. The Smart Guides that are on as default should help you. If the Smart Guides are not active, choose View > Smart Guides. Note that if Smart Guides is already checked, they are on.

The saved shape is available as a custom shape.

Once you have repositioned the SNOWBIRD text, you will need to expand the Illustrator artboard to fit the new art.

6   Double-click the Artboard tool (▦) from the Illustrator tools panel. The Artboard Options dialog box appears.

7   From the Preset drop-down menu, select Fit Artwork Bounds and click OK. The artboard now fits the new position of the artwork.

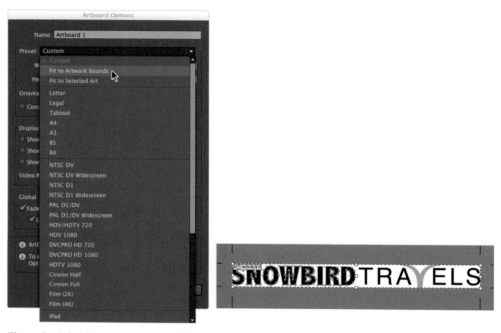

Change the Artboard Options to fit Artwork bounds.   The artboard changes to fit the artwork.

8   Choose File > Save, and then File > Close.

9   Return to Photoshop to see that the artwork for the logo is automatically updated.

10 Select the Move tool and reposition the text and the logo to better fit into the image. No exact position is necessary.

11 Click the Visibility icon (👁) of your Rectangle 1 layer so you can see the full image composition.

12 Choose File > Save. Keep your file open for the last part of this lesson.

Saving your file for use outside of Photoshop

If you want to keep your artwork and text in vector form, you should keep your file in the Photoshop format. You can choose File > Place to import native Photoshop files into most of the other Adobe Creative Cloud applications. If you are saving to an application outside of the Creative Cloud, you might have to choose a different format.

In the last section of this lesson, you'll save your file as a Photoshop PDF.

1   Choose File > Save As. When the Save As dialog box appears, choose Photoshop PDF from the Format drop-down menu. Type the file name **advps09_logo2** into the Name text field and make sure that you are saving into the advps09lesson folder. Leave all other options at the default settings, and then click Save. If a warning appears about the PDF Settings, click OK. The Save Adobe PDF dialog box appears.

2   Choose the Adobe PDF Preset of High Quality Print. Leave all other settings at the default settings, and then click Save PDF.

    If you see a warning about Preserving Photoshop Editing Capabilities, click the check box that indicates that you do not want to show the dialog box again, and then click Yes.

    To test that the vector artwork has been maintained, you will choose to open the saved PDF file in Adobe Illustrator.

3   Return to Adobe Illustrator and choose File > Open. Navigate to the advps09lessons folder and select the **advps09_logo2.pdf** file that you just saved.

4   Use your Selection tool to click and select the various vector objects that you created in Adobe Photoshop. Note that the vectors remained editable, even in the PDF format.

5   Choose File > Close to close your image in Adobe Illustrator. You do not have to save any changes.

6   Return to Adobe Photoshop and choose File > Close.

Self Study

You can experiment with vectors objects in Adobe Photoshop in several ways. From this lesson, you learned the following:

- To create a vector shape and use Photoshop effects on that shape.
- To copy and paste vector art from other applications.
- To create images with text that remains vector.
- To convert text to a vector shape.
- To import Illustrator artwork as a Smart Object.

Practice your new skills by applying at least three of them to the extra vector images (beach related) found in the advps09lessons folder.

Review

Questions

1 What is the benefit to using vector shapes in Photoshop?

2 What feature would you use to bring a multicolored illustrator object into Photoshop?

3 How can you add a custom shape?

Answers

1 The benefit of using vector shapes is that they are scalable and remain editable objects as long as they are not rasterized, or saved in a format that does not support vectors.

2 To bring in artwork and keep all the color and stroke properties, you would choose File > Place.

3 You can add any path as a custom shape. This includes one that you might have created directly in Photoshop using the Pen tool. You can also choose to Copy and Paste a path from Adobe Illustrator. Then choose Edit > Define Custom shape.

Lesson 10

What you'll learn in this lesson:

- Determining the optimum file size
- Deciding on the best format
- Exporting optimized images from Photoshop
- Slicing images in Photoshop

Creating Images for the Web and Application Design

In this lesson, you'll learn how to optimize images for display on screen, whether in a web browser or on a device. By learning about the different image formats, you'll be able to export files that contain accurate colors and transparency if needed. You'll also discover image slicing and how you can choose different formats for parts of a single image.

Starting up

Before starting, make sure that your tools and panels are consistent by resetting your preferences. See "Resetting Adobe Photoshop CC preferences" in the Starting up section of this book. You will work with several files from the advps10lessons folder in this lesson. Make sure that you have loaded the advpslessons folder onto your hard drive from the supplied DVD. For more information, see "Loading lesson files" in the Starting up section of this book.

See Lesson 10 in action!

Use the accompanying video to gain a better understanding of how to use some of the features shown in this lesson. You can find the video tutorial for this lesson on the included DVD.

Optimizing graphics for on-screen presentation

Optimizing refers to the preparation of images for use as assets for applications or in websites. The goal of optimization is to reduce the file size of the image for faster downloading, without compromising the quality of the image. Ultimately, you might have to reduce the quality of your images so they are small enough to be downloaded and viewed quickly; in many cases, it is more important to have a speedy download than to make the user wait for beautiful (but large) image files.

Before you start adjusting the file size of your images, you should have a general idea of how you will use them and how big they will be.

Resizing the image

Many designers mistakenly believe that if an image has a resolution of 72 dpi (dots per inch), it's ready for the Web. However, the *total pixel dimensions* of the image is much more important.

In this part of the lesson, you will discover some facts about resizing your images in Photoshop.

1   In Adobe Photoshop, choose File > Open. Navigate to the advps10lessons folder and open the file named **advps1001.psd**. An image of several people enjoying smoothies appears.

The designer has planned well and knows the approximate size that this image will be on the web page. You will now open the low fidelity wireframe that the designer created to plan the size of the image within the page.

2   Keep the file **advps1001.psd** open, and choose File > Open. In the dialog box that appears, navigate to the advps10lessons folder.

3   Locate the image named **advps1002.jpg** and click Open. The wireframe appears.

The rough design for this web page.

In this example, the size of the screen is approximately 800 pixels wide. For more information about browser windows and sizes, see the sidebar, "Images and browser window size." The images you will work on are represented by the two solid squares on the right.

In this case, you have a mock-up that helps to determine the size of the final images. Even if you do not have a mock-up prepared before optimizing your images, you should know the approximate size of your final images based on the final size of the web page.

Images and browser window size

According to the website *Counter.com*, over 50 percent of users have monitors with a resolution of 1024×768 pixels. Thirty percent have 1280×1024-pixel monitors. This does not mean their browser window opens to that size; in fact, their browser window usually varies from 800×600 pixels to 960×600 pixels.

To determine how wide a web image should be, separate the total number of screen pixels into sections, and specify the percentage of the screen you want the image to occupy. For example, if you want the image to occupy half the screen (remember, browser windows are typically about 900 pixels across), type **480** into the Width text field in the Pixel Dimensions section of the Image Size dialog box; for one-quarter of the screen, type **240**, and so on. You should also remember that the pixel size will not change, regardless of the ppi resolution of your image. So, 200 pixels in a 300-ppi image occupy as much window space as 200 pixels in a 72-ppi image.

At this point, you can determine the approximate size of the optimized images. In this example, you will use the grid feature separated into percentages to help you determine the size of the images.

4 With **advps1002.jpg** open, choose View > Show > Grid. A grid appears in the image area. You will now adjust the grid size and units of measurement.

5 Choose Edit > Preferences > Units and Rulers (Windows) or Photoshop > Preferences > Units and Rulers (Mac OS).

6 Select Pixels from the Ruler drop-down menu.

7 Before exiting the Preferences dialog box, choose Guides, Grids & Slices from the list of items on the left side.

8 In the Grid section of the Guides, Grids & Slices dialog box, type **100** in the Gridline Every text field and choose percent from the drop-down menu.

9 In the Subdivisions text field, type **8** and click OK.

Each of the four grid subdivisions represents 100 pixels; you can use this value to determine the size you want to optimize your image to.

Set up the grid lines to appear in eight subdivisions.

Adjusting the image size

By looking at the grid sections on your mock-up, you can see that the images on the right are approximately 225 pixels wide by 150 pixels high.

If you have Photoshop Extended, you can select an area in your image, choose Window > Measurement, and then click the Record Measurements button to see the pixel dimensions of your selection. This is a helpful feature when trying to rebuild from existing compositions.

You will now optimize this image to fit the allotted space. First, you'll check the file size of this image.

1   Return to the **advps1001.psd** file and select Image > Image Size. The Image Size dialog box appears.

2   If the unit of measurement is not set to pixels, change the measurement to pixels. The size indicates that this file is 786 pixels wide by 567 pixels high.

The Image Size dialog box.

On-screen images cannot accommodate more dots per inch in the same space; they occupy space on the monitor based on their pixel count. This particular image would use about 90 percent of a browser window as calculated from the pixel dimensions, not from the resolution. In the following steps, you will only consider pixel dimensions.

3   After looking at the pixel information in the Image Size dialog box, click Cancel. Since you must determine a specific width and height, you will use the Crop tool.

4   Click the Crop tool (⌖) to select it in the Tools panel.

5 In the Options bar select W x H x Resolution from the Select a preset aspect ratio or crop size. Type **225px** in the Width text field and **150px** in the Height text field. Note that entering a pixel value for resolution is unnecessary as the size is determined by your pixel values for Width and Height.

Fix the crop size.

6 With the Crop tool still selected, click and drag to select the area you want to include in the final image; no exact area is necessary for this lesson. Notice that you cannot control the proportions of your crop; you are forced to use the same proportions as the pixel amounts you entered.

Crop the image to a fixed pixel size.

7 Once you determine the crop area, press Enter or Return, or click the checkmark icon (✔) in the upper-right corner of the Options bar. Since the resolution is reduced, your image file shrinks in its view size.

If you want to cancel a crop, press the Esc key or click the Cancel Current Crop Operation button (⊘), also in the upper-right corner of the Control panel.

8 Choose Image > Image Size; in the Image Size dialog box, you see that the image area is now cropped to the required dimensions.

Applying the Unsharp Mask filter to an image

We recommend that you sharpen an image after resizing it, since resizing the image can cause it to become blurry. The following figure shows the image before and after the Unsharp feature is applied. The Unsharp Mask feature sharpens the image based on levels of contrast, while keeping the areas that don't have contrasting pixels smooth. In this lesson, you will apply Unsharp Masking using a Smart filter.

An example of an image before (left) and after (right) unsharp masking is applied.

Follow these steps to apply the Unsharp Mask filter:

1   Choose View > 100% or double-click the Zoom tool (🔍).

When you're using any filter, you should view your image at actual size to see the results more clearly.

2   Choose > Filter > Convert for Smart Filters. If a Warning dialog box appears click OK. Your Background is converted to Layer 0 and is a Smart Object.

3   Choose Filter > Sharpen > Unsharp Mask.

The Unsharp Mask dialog box displays three settings:

Amount: The Amount value ranges from 0 to 500. The amount you choose depends upon the subject matter. For example, you can sharpen a car or appliance at 300 or 400, but with a portrait, every wrinkle, mole, or hair will become more defined. If you are unsure about the value to use, start with 150 and gradually increase the amount until you find a value that looks good.

Radius: The Unsharp Mask filter creates a halo around the areas that have enough contrast to be considered an edge. For print images, you can use a value between 1 and 2, but if you're creating a billboard or poster, increase the size.

Threshold: The Threshold value is the most important one in the Unsharp Mask dialog box because it determines the parts of the image that should be sharpened. This value can range from 0 to 255. Apply too much, and no sharpening appears; apply too little, and the image becomes grainy. For example, if you leave it at zero, noise appears throughout the image, much like the grain you see in high-speed film. A value of 10 causes the filter to apply when the pixels are ten shades or more away from each other. Start with a value of 10, and gradually increase it until you find a value that works well.

4 For this exercise, set the Amount to **200**, Radius to **.5**, and Threshold to **10**.

You can compare the original image with the resulting image in the Preview pane of the Unsharp Mask dialog box by clicking and holding the image in the Preview pane; this shows the original state of the image. When you release the mouse button, you preview the Unsharp Mask filter again.

5 Click OK to apply the filter. The image is sharpened.

6 Choose File > Save; keep the file open for the next part of this lesson.

In some images, stray colored pixels might appear after you apply the Unsharp Mask filter. If this occurs in your image, choose the Double-click to edit filter blending options button (🗲) to the right of Unsharp Mask in the Layers panel. In the Blending Mode dialog box, select the Luminosity blend mode from the Mode drop-down list and then click OK. This step applies the Unsharp Mask filter to the grays in the image only, thereby eliminating sharpening of colored pixels.

Selecting the best image format

When saving an image that you will use on the Web or in other devices, you need to consider two factors: the quality and size of the image file. When you are saving a file, you must find a balance between the quality you want and the download speed your viewers demand.

In this section, you will look at different file formats and decide on a format for the picture you just resized. The following example uses the Save for Web feature in Adobe Photoshop.

Choosing the right file format

The most popular formats for web images are JPEG, PNG, and GIF. Each one of these formats has benefits and drawbacks, as shown in the following table.

File Formats

File Format	Lossy	Supports Anti-Aliasing	Supports Transparency	Supports Animations	Supports Varying Amounts Of Transparency	Has Limited Colors	Is Best For Photos	Is Best For Solid Colors
JPEG	•	•					•	
PNG-8	•				•	•		•
PNG-24	•	•	•		•		•	•
GIF			•	•		•		•

Choosing the best file format for your image

Throughout this lesson, you will have the opportunity to save images in each of the major file formats: JPEG, PNG, and GIF. You will also see the differences between the formats and when to use each.

Saving images as JPEGs

The JPEG file format helps you keep the image size down, but some loss in image quality occurs when you save the image file. Since the JPEG format supports anti-aliasing, it is typically recommended for photographic images and illustrations with gradients. (Anti-aliasing is a technique used in computer graphics that helps smooth out the naturally jagged edges of objects such as text or any area where a transition in tonal values is needed.) When saving an image as a JPEG, you can choose varying levels of quality.

Choosing the quality of a JPEG

In the following steps, you will complete the optimization process by saving your image as a JPEG.

1   With **advps1001.psd** still open, choose File > Save for Web. The Save for Web window appears.

The Save for Web window allows you to preview changes that you make in the settings, such as file type and size. The section in the upper-right corner of the window is where you determine the file format and file compression settings. In this example, JPEG is selected.

The Save for Web feature is used here to create an image for the Web but you can also use this feature to prepare and preview files for use on mobile devices and for application design.

Above the Format drop-down menu is the Preset drop-down menu. This menu contains pre-configured settings for many file formats. Later in this lesson you will learn how to store your own presets in this menu.

In the upper-left corner is a toolbar with tools you can use to select sections (or slices) of an image, zoom into, and sample colors from an image.

The large preview window allows you to compare different file formats and compression settings. You can compare up to four file formats and see the approximate download times and file sizes.

2   Select the 2-Up tab at the top of the preview window.

3 Click to select the second image preview to assign settings.

From the Preset drop-down menu, select JPEG High. Note that the image preview shows an image of the file in that format and displays information about the JPEG settings in the lower-left corner.

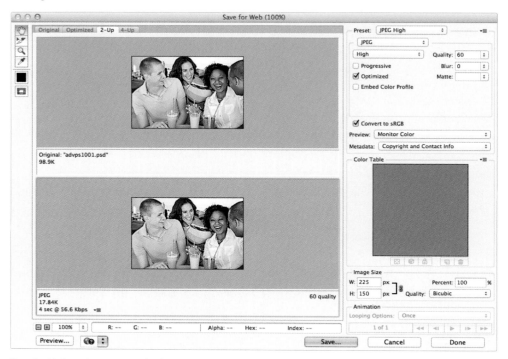

Download information appears under the preview.

In this example, the file is reduced to 17.84K and it will take about 4 seconds to download at the speed of about 56.6 kbps (kilobits per second).

You can change the speed and recalculate the download time by clicking the Select Download Speed button (▾≡) located to the right of the download speed.

You will lower the image quality in the following steps to reduce the file size.

4 Click the Compression quality drop-down menu located below the Format drop-down menu and choose Medium; note that the settings change along with the download information. The JPEG image format uses lossy compression to save a file. Lossy means that the image is compressed by discarding part of the data in the file.

5 Click the Compression quality drop-down menu and choose Low. The visual quality changes and the download time decreases.

For this example, the Low quality is too low and the download time for Medium quality is too long. Toggle between the two settings to see that the Quality text field indicates that Low is set to 10 and Medium is set to 30. These presets are helpful, but you can manually adjust the settings.

6 Click Quality to display the Quality slider and drag it to the right, increasing the value to **20**.

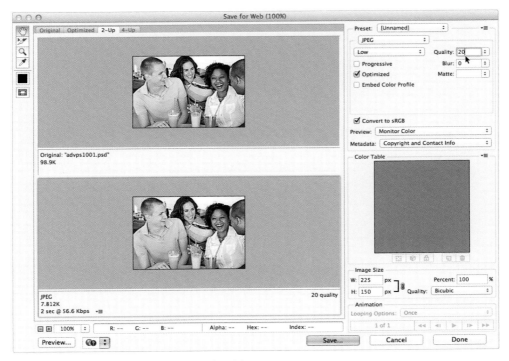

Customize the quality of your image using the Quality slider.

Previewing your image

The Save for Web window allows you to preview an image file in a browser before saving it. You must first ensure that a browser can be recognized from this window.

1 Click the Preview the Optimized Image in a Browser button (⬛), which will have a question mark beside it if you have not selected a browser, and choose Edit List.

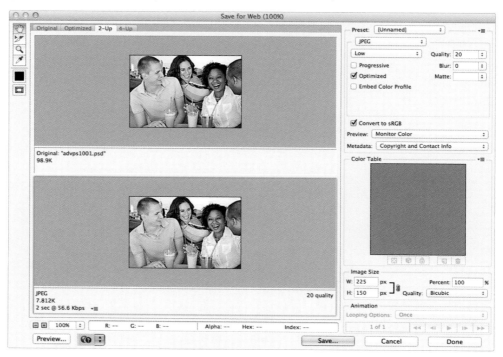

To choose a web browser, click the Preview the Optimized Image in a Browser button.

2 When the browser window appears, click Add. In the dialog box that appears, navigate to C:\Program Files (Windows) or Macintosh HD\Applications (Mac OS) and locate the browser in which you want to preview your images. Click Open and then click OK in the browser window.

3 Click the Preview button to view your image in the browser. If you want to change the quality, close the browser window and return to the Save for Web window.

4 To improve the image quality, change the JPEG setting to Very High. Preview the image directly in the Save for Web window.

5 Click Save in the Save for Web window. In the dialog box that appears, navigate to the advps10lessons folder.

6 Name the file **advps1001_optimized**, and make sure that Images only is selected in the Format drop-down menu.

7 Make sure Settings are configured to Default Settings, and then click Save. Remember that when creating a website, you should save this image file into the appropriate site folder.

You are now back to your image in Photoshop. It is strongly recommend that you keep a copy of your image in an uncompressed format such as the Photoshop native format (PSD). Avoid saving a file multiple times as a JPEG, because the quality is reduced every time you save your file in this lossy format.

8 Choose File > Save As and navigate to the advps10lessons folder. In the File Name text field, type **advps1001_done**. Choose the Photoshop (PSD) format, and click Save.

9 Choose File > Close to close the file.

Creating a transparency effect in a JPEG image

Transparency doesn't exist in the JPEG format, but you can simulate the transparency effect.

In following steps, you will use the Matting feature to match the background color of your web page and then preview the image in your browser.

1 Choose File > Open. In the dialog box that appears, navigate to the advps10lessons folder, select the image named **advps1003.psd**, and click Open. An image of a smoothie with a transparent background appears.

When you save an image for the Web or for application design, file size is a big concern. Since this is a photographic image, JPEG is the best format to use to keep the file size small. However, the web page has a pale yellow background, and by default, the JPEG will appear with a white background. The solution is to use the Matte control, which becomes available when you optimize this file.

2 Choose File > Save for Web. In the Save for Web window, choose JPEG Medium from the Preset drop-down menu.

3 Selected the Optimized tab so that you see only the optimized file.

4 Click the Matte drop-down menu and choose Other. The Color Picker appears.

5 In the Hexadecimal text field (located to the right of the # sign), type **FFFFCC**; then click OK. The color appears immediately in the preview window.

6 Click the Preview button to preview the image in the browser with the new matte color applied.

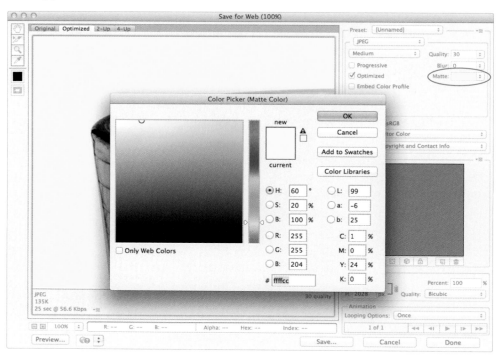

Preview your image in a web browser with the background color applied.

7 Close your browser window and return to the Save for Web window.

Saving your settings

You can store your customized settings for future use through the Optimize Panel menu in the upper-right corner of the Optimize section of the Save for Web window. Follow these steps to store your settings:

1   With the Save for Web window still open, click the Optimize Panel menu in the upper-right corner of the Optimize section, and select Save Settings. The Save Optimization Settings dialog box appears.

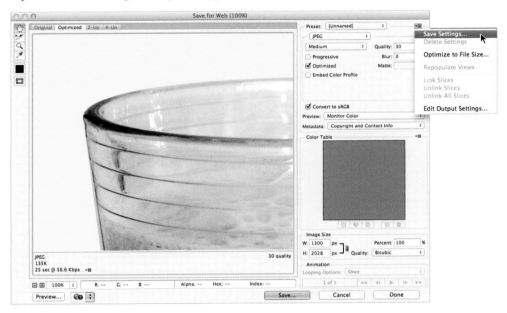

Save your custom settings.

You are automatically directed to the Optimized Settings folder for your application. To share this setting, browse to a location on a server or removable device.

2   In the Save As text field, type **JPEG_ffffcc**, and then click Save. You now can select these settings from the Preset drop-down menu at the top of the Optimize window.

Now that you have saved your settings, you will save your optimized image file.

3   In the Save for Web window, click Save. In the dialog box that appears, navigate to the advps10lessons folder and in the File Name text field, type **advps1003_optimized**. Ensure that the Format menu is set to Images Only and that the Settings menu is set to Default Settings. Click Save, then select File > Close.

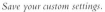

To test a file, click Done instead of Save. This keeps your settings and does not save the file.

Saving images as GIFs

GIF is a popular web format that has limitations in terms of color and appearance. This file format is lossless, so the clarity of the image is not compromised by GIF compression. You can compress the file size of a GIF by reducing the image's pixel dimensions and the number of indexed colors that it uses, which makes GIF the best format for images with a lot of solid colors, such as logos and illustrations. The compression algorithms for GIF files work best on large spans of color, thereby reducing the file size when optimized. However, a photographic image or an illustration with a lot of tonal values will result in a much larger file size than a same-sized image with solid colors.

The GIF format works best with images that have large spans of solid colors. In this example, an image with a lot of tonal values are saved as a GIF with 32 colors.

When saving as a GIF, your image file can contain up to 256 indexed colors, but you should reduce the number of colors to the minimum. You can reduce an image to four colors, but it requires testing to find the best-looking file with the smallest file size.

You can animate GIF files and include transparent pixels to blend the image with different-colored backgrounds. The pixels in a GIF image must be fully transparent or fully opaque, so you cannot fade the transparency as with a PNG image, which is discussed later in this lesson.

In the following steps, you will open an image that contains multiple shades of solid color, and you will save it with a transparent background. You will then animate the image.

You should use animations conservatively because many viewers do not like the distraction.

1   Choose File > Open. In the dialog box that appears, browse to the advps10lessons
     folder and open the file named **advps1004.psd**. A colorful logo appears.

The logo you will optimize.

This logo contains a large amount of solid color, and has an image behind it. In such
situations you must determine the part of the image on which you want to focus; in
this case, you will focus on the logo type, not the image behind it.

You will now remove the background. When you have a solid background, you can
remove it using the Magic Eraser tool, which has a tolerance option to control the
pixels to delete to transparency.

2   Select the Magic Eraser tool (✐), which is hidden under the Eraser tool (✐) in the
     Tools panel.

3   In the Options bar at the top of the window, confirm that the number 32 is in the
     Tolerance text field. Also, make sure that the Contiguous option is checked.

Tolerance determines how much of a selected pixel color is deleted when you use the
Magic Eraser tool: the higher the value, the more shades of that color are deleted. The
lower the value, the fewer shades of that color are deleted. Selecting the Contiguous
option ensures that only touching pixels are deleted to transparency.

Click the Contiguous button to select only pixels that are connected to each other.

4   Click the White background. The Background layer converts to Layer 0 and the
     background becomes transparent.

5   Choose File > Save as, and in the dialog box that appears, navigate to the
     advps10lessons folder. Name the file **advps1004_work**, and keep it in the Photoshop
     PSD format. Click Save. Keep the file open for the next part of this lesson.

Optimizing the GIF image

In the following steps, you will determine the best settings for optimizing your GIF image. You will use a color table to affect the appearance of the final optimized image.

1 With the **advps1004_work** image still open, choose Image > Image Size. In the Image Size dialog box, change the Width to **200** pixels and click OK.

2 Your image might appear smaller on the screen than it actually is. Double-click the Zoom tool (🔍) to view your image at 100 percent.

3 Choose File > Save for Web. The Save for Web window appears.

4 Choose GIF 64 No Dither from the Preset drop-down menu, and select the Transparency check box. Notice in the GIF preview that the image size is now about 10K.

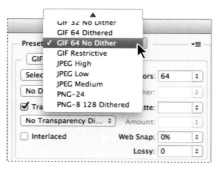

Select a GIF preset.

Understanding dithering

Dithering is the attempt to approximate a color from a mixture of other colors when the required color is not available. Dithering produces a pattern or grainy appearance in images, and you should only use it to help define tonal values.

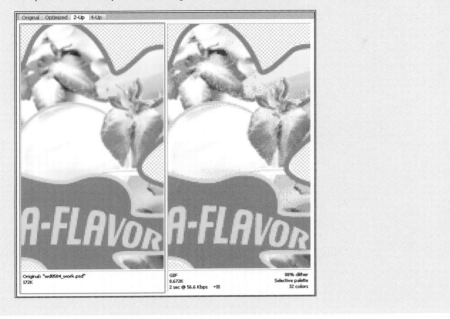

5   Keep this window open for the next part of this lesson.

Using the color table

By selecting GIF 64 No Dither, you have indicated that you want to use 64 colors in your optimized image. Note that the color table in the optimization section displays a table of these indexed colors.

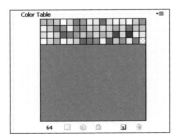

Use the color table to keep the most important colors in your image.

You can delete, change, or lock the colors in this table to preserve the look of your image. In this section, you will learn to lock critical colors to make sure important colors are not deleted when you reduce the number of colors in the table.

1   With the image still open in the Save for Web window, select the Eyedropper tool (✐) and click the orange color surrounding the text in the optimized GIF preview of the image. The Eyedropper samples the color and selects that color in the color table to the right. This tool is useful when you need to ensure that a specific color appears as close as possible to the print color. For example, the logo for this exercise might be for a company where the branding department wants to ensure the specific orange used appears as close as possible to the print color (PMS 173 for this example).

Use the Eyedropper tool to select a color from the optimized image.

The Pantone Color Matching System (PMS) is a standardized color reproduction system used mostly in print, but whose colors can also be used online. By standardizing colors, corporations can ensure their colors stay as consistent as possible regardless of where the colors are reproduced.

2   Locate the selected color in the color table and double-click it to open the Color Picker. You can use the Color Picker to enter a new value for the selected color.

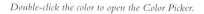

Double-click the color to open the Color Picker.

In the Color Picker window, you can specify colors in any color space; for example, you could choose an RGB or Hexadecimal value. For this lesson, you will closely match a Pantone color a client has provided to you.

Type Hexadecimal values in the text field to the right of the # sign.

3   Click the Color Libraries button to open the Color Libraries window. The Pantone solid coated library is selected by default. Each color in this library represents a specific Pantone color on coated paper. The color is automatically matched with the most similar Pantone color.

Open the Color Libraries section of the Color Picker.

Return to the standard Color Picker by clicking the Picker button.

4   In this example, the client has specified that the orange should match PMS 173. Click the color value Pantone 173 C, and then click OK. The color changes to match the value of PMS 173 and has a white square icon in the lower-right corner with a diagonal line through it. This indicates that the color is locked and was mapped to a color other than the original. You will now lock additional colors.

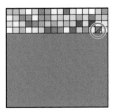

This color was locked and mapped to a specific value.

5   Click any color in the color table, and then click the padlock icon (🔒) at the bottom of the color table. For this part of the exercise, select four additional colors you would like to retain in this image, and lock them as instructed in the previous steps.

You will now reduce the number of color values in the optimized image even further.

6   From the Colors drop-down menu, choose 8. This is a significant reduction in the number of colors, and although your important colors are locked and the file size has been reduced, the image quality is poor. You will need to increase the number of colors used to improve the quality.

Reduce the color values in the color table.

7   Using the Colors drop-down menu, increase the number to 32. Keep this window open for the next part of the lesson.

Adding a matte to a GIF

When placing images over a colored background, you might see a pixelated edge. You can avoid this edge by applying matting to the image in the optimization stage. Matting lets you to find pixels that are almost transparent. However, unlike pixels in PNG images, pixels in a GIF image are either transparent or not. In the following steps, you will apply matting that matches the background color of the web page where the image will be placed.

1   With the Save for Web window still open, click the white section in the Matte drop-down menu. The Color Picker appears.

Select a custom matting color.

2   In the Color Picker window, type **3366CC** into the Hexadecimal text field (located to the right of the # sign). Click OK. Notice that the graphic now has a thin, dark-blue border around the edge. If you choose to use this image on a page with a different background, remember to change the matting color to match the new background.

Matting applied to the GIF image.

3   Test your image by clicking the Preview button at the bottom of the Save for Web window. The preview window matches the matting color you selected so you can see the image in the same background color in the browser.

4   Once you are done previewing your file, close the browser, return to the Save for Web window, and click Save. In the Save As dialog box, browse to locate the advps10lessons folder. Name the file **advps1004_optimized.gif**, and then click Save.

5   Choose File > Close to close the **advps1004_work** file.

Animating a GIF

Where appropriate, animated GIFs add interest to a web page. In the following steps, you will create an animated GIF.

1   In Adobe Photoshop, choose File > Open. In the Open dialog box, locate the image named **advps1005.psd** in the advps10lessons folder. The original image file for the last image you worked on is now open.

2   Choose File > Save As, and in the Save As dialog box type **advps1005_work** into the File name text field. Make sure that you are saving the file into the advps10lessons folder and that it is still in the native Photoshop format. Click Save.

3 Choose Window > Timeline to open the Timeline panel. If necessary, select Create
Frame Animation from the Create Video Timeline, and then click the Create Frame
Animation button, the Timeline panel shows your initial frame for the animation.

The Animation panel in the Timeline mode.

The Animation panel in the Frames mode.

In Photoshop, frames are like a flip book. Each frame appears for the amount of time you
specify, creating a simple animation.

4 In the Animation panel, select the duplicates selected frames icon (⬛) to duplicate
your frame.

5 Select the Move tool, and then select the Pick-A-Flavor layer. Click and drag the
Pick-A-Flavor logo to the bottom of the image area.

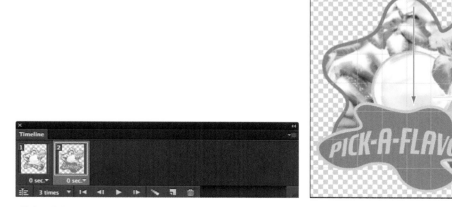

Click and drag the Pick-a-Flavor layer to reposition it in the second frame.

6   Click the first frame in the Animation panel; the original position is intact in this frame. Click the second frame; the logo appears repositioned to the bottom of the image area.

Changing the timing of an animation

The timing of the animation is important. In the following steps, you will change the speed at which the frames are viewed, and also change the number of times they rotate through the flip.

1   Select both frames by clicking the first frame and Shift+clicking the second frame in the Animation panel.

2   Click the arrow in the lower-right corner of either frame to open the frame delay time. If it is not already set, choose 0.1 second. You will now change the number of times your animation will play.

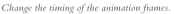

Change the timing of the animation frames.

3   Click the Selects Looping Options (Once) button in the lower-left corner of the Animation panel and change the value to 3 times. The animation will now play three times and then stop.

Changing additional properties in an animation

You will now change the opacity value of the Pick-A-Flavor layer. A layer that has a value of 100 percent opacity is completely visible. A layer that has a value of 0 percent opacity is not visible. You will now set different opacity values for the first two frames to create an "off/on" visual effect.

1   Select the first frame in the Animation panel, and then select the Pick-A-Flavor layer in the Layers panel. Click and drag the Opacity slider from 100 percent to 0 percent.

Change the opacity of the frames.

2   Click the second frame, and with the same Pick-A-Flavor layer selected, drag the Opacity slider to the right until it reaches 100 percent.

3   Test the animation by clicking the Play button (▶) at the bottom of the Animation panel. A flashy animation plays three times. In the following steps, you will use the Tween feature to create a better transition between the frames.

Tweening

In the following steps, you will build a better transition between the frames. Tweening automatically creates new frames between two existing frames. The process saves you the time and the effort from having to make each frame manually.

1   Select any frame, and then click the tweens animation frames icon (◔) at the bottom of the Animation panel. The Tween window appears.

2   In the Tween window, type **5** into the Frames to add text field. Leave the others settings at their defaults, and click OK. Three frames are added in between the existing frames.

Tween		
Tween With:	Previous Frame ⬍	OK
Frames to Add:	5	Cancel

Layers
⦿ All Layers
◯ Selected Layers

Parameters
☑ Position
☑ Opacity
☑ Effects

Create a smooth transition by using the Tween feature.

3   Click the plays animation icon (▶) to test your animation.

4   Choose File > Save for Web and make sure the setting for Preset is GIF 64 No Dither. Then click Save.

5   In the Save Optimized dialog box, leave the name the same and choose the advps10lessons folder for the destination, and then click Save.

6   Choose File > Close to close the file.

Saving as a PNG

Some characteristics, such as the ability to display variable levels of transparency, are uniquely supported by the PNG format, but you cannot reduce the file size such as you can with JPEG and GIF formats. You can use the PNG format to benefit from its unique characteristics more than for a need to reduce file size.

In the following steps, you will create a navigation bar.

1   Choose File > Open, and in the Open dialog box, select the file named **advps1006.psd**. You will use this image at the top of a web page.

The initial artwork.

2 In the Layers panel there are three layers already created. You will first group these layers, and then apply a mask to all three layers to allow the image to fade from 100 percent to 0 percent opacity.

3 Select the bottom layer (baseimage) and Shift+click the top layer (Get Healthy). All three layers are now selected.

4 From the Layers panel menu, choose New Group from Layers. The New Group from Layers dialog box appears. Type **banner** in the Name text field, and then click OK.

Choose to group the layers.

5 Click the Add layer mask (⬛) button at the bottom of the Layers panel. A mask is added to the entire group of layers you created.

Add a mask to the banner group.

6   Select the Gradient tool (■) from the Tools panel and press **D**. This restores the foreground and background colors to their defaults (black and white).

7   Click the Gradient Picker in the Options bar and make sure you have the Foreground to Background gradient selected.

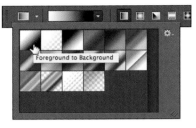

Make sure that the Foreground to Background gradient is selected.

8   Using the Gradient tool, click and drag from the letter y in the word healthy to the right side of the image. Press and hold the Shift key while dragging to constrain the Gradient tool to a straight line.

Click and drag with the Gradient tool across the image area.   *A gradient has been added to the mask.*

By creating a mask for the group and applying a gradient to it, you have created a gradient mask that fades the banner layers to 0 percent opacity.

9   Choose File > Save for Web. When the Save for Web window appears, choose
PNG-24 from the Preset drop-down menu. PNG-24 supports varying levels of
transparency in the image.

Select PNG-24 to use the fade to transparency feature.

10 Click the Preview button at the bottom of the Save for Web window to see a preview
of your PNG file in a browser.

11 Once you have previewed your image, close the browser window and return to the
Save for Web window.

12 Click Save. In the dialog box that appears, browse to the advps10lessons folder, name
the file **advps1006_banner.png**, and click Save. Choose File > Save, and then File >
Close to close the file.

PNG-8 versus PNG-24

Many software packages allow you to save an image in PNG-8 or PNG-24 format. The 8
and 24 represent the number of bits each file format contains. The one you choose depends
on the type of image and how you want it to appear. The PNG-8 format uses an indexed
color palette similar to GIFs, which makes this format ideal for images with areas of solid,
even colors. Use the PNG-24 format when you want variable transparency or many gradients
in your image.

Slicing an image

In this section, you will learn to slice an image in Adobe Photoshop. A slice is a part of an image, cut from a larger image. These pieces are held together by an HTML table or Cascading Style Sheets (CSS). In this example, you will use CSS to create the final navigation bar.

An example of a sliced image.

Slices are useful when your web page contains large images, because downloading several smaller packets of information on the Web is faster than downloading one large packet. Slices are also helpful when you need to save parts of an image in different formats. In this exercise, you will use existing layers to create slices. Note that you can also use guides to determine where the slicing of your image occurs.

Viewing the completed file

Before starting this lesson, you'll use your browser to view the completed image with navigational links that you will create in this section.

1   Open your web browser.

2   Choose File > Open, or the Open file command appropriate for your specific browser.

This page is created using CSS; you can export pages built from tables of CSS from the Photoshop Save for Web window. Find out more about CSS at w3.org/Style/CSS/.

3   In the Open dialog box, navigate to the advps10lessons folder and open the sitefolder located inside. Choose to open the **index.html** file. An image created to help viewers navigate a website appears.

ABOUT	RECIPES	BOOKS	STORE

You have reached the Index page

The completed navigation bar in a web browser.

4   Click the ABOUT, RECIPES, BOOKS, and STORE text links; these links take you to generic pages with related titles. As you can see, each slice can have its own independent attributes, such as file type and link.

You will create this web page from start to finish, including adding the links, and export the page using CSS.

5   You can keep the finished web page open in the browser for reference, or choose File > Close.

6   Return to Photoshop.

Creating slices

You will now use the existing layers in this image to create layer-based slices using Adobe Photoshop.

You will start by saving a work file.

1   Choose File > Open and browse to the advps10lessons folder. Open the file named **advps1007.psd**. The navigational banner appears.

2   Choose File > Save as. In the Save As dialog box, type **advps1007_work.psd** into the Name text field. Make sure that you are saving into the advps10lessons folder, and then click Save.

3   Choose Window > Layers to open the Layers panel if it is not already visible.

4   Select the Slice Select tool (✂), which is hidden under the Crop tool.

5   Select the About Shape layer, press and hold the Shift key, and click the Store Shape layer. All four shape layers are now selected.

6   Choose Layer > New Layer Based Slices. The shape layers are now defined as slices.

7   Choose File > Save; keep this file open for the next section.

Changing the attributes of the slices

In the following steps, you will change the individual slice attributes to add alternative text and individual hyperlinks.

1   Using the Slice Select tool, which is hidden under the Slice tool, make sure no slices are active by clicking between any two slices.

*You cannot have any slices selected before changing
individual attributes of the slices.*

2   Using the Slice Select tool (✂), select the About Slice, and then click the Set Options for the Current Slice button (▤), which is located in the upper-right corner of the Options bar. The Slice Options window appears.

3   In the Name text field, type **about**.

4   In the URL text field, type **about.html**. To create a link to an existing page, you would type the URL address here. To allow the user to navigate to an external link, you would enter a full address. For this exercise, you are linking to a local page located inside the same folder where you will be saving this sliced image.

5   In the Alt Tag text field, type **About**. The text in the Alt Tag text field is visible to users when they place their mouse cursor over the link, or choose to not have the graphics on the web page visible. An accurate Alt tag also gives search engines more information about your web page. Click OK.

Changing the first slice's options.

6   With the Slice Select tool, click the Recipes slice, and then click the Set Options for the Current Slice button (▤).

7   Type **recipes** into the Name text field, **recipes.html** into the URL text field, and **Recipes** into the Alt Tag text field. Click OK.

8   Continue this process by double-clicking the third slice, Books. (Double-clicking a slice is another way to open the Slice Options dialog box.) In the Slice Options dialog box, type **books** in the name text field, **books.html** in the URL text field, and **Books** in the Alt Tag text field; then click OK.

9   Repeat this process for the Store slice, typing **store** in the Name text field, **store.html** in the URL text field, and **Store** in the Alt Tag text field. Then click OK.

10   Choose File > Save to save this file. Keep it open for the next part of this lesson.

You are now ready to optimize these images and create your HTML page.

Saving slices out of Photoshop

In this section, you will learn to optimize your sliced images and save them to an HTML file that contains the code needed to create the final navigation bar on a web page.

1 With the **advps1007_work.psd** file still open, choose File > Save for Web.

2 In the Save for Web window, choose the Slice Select tool from the toolbar in the upper-left corner, and click each slice once. Note that you can choose a different optimization setting for each slice. This is useful for images that have a lot of gradients in one section and solid colors in another.

3 Click the About slice, and then Shift+click the Recipes, Books, and Store slices. All the slices are now selected.

4 Choose PNG-8 from the Optimized File Format drop-down menu, since this image only has a few solid colors.

5 Choose Perceptual for the Color reduction algorithm, which creates a custom color table by giving priority to colors for which the human eye has greater sensitivity.

6 Choose No Dither from the Specify the Dithering Algorithm drop-down menu. Dithering scatters different colored pixels throughout an image to make it appear as though there are more colors than are actually present. This can result in a grainy appearance in your solid spans of color.

7 Choose 16 from the Colors drop-down menu. The image used for this exercise appears to have two colors, blue and white, but it has more. Transparency is a color, and the transition between the white text and the blue background contains many shades of color. If you reduce the colors too much, you will have a pixelated result.

8 Select the Transparency check box.

A portion of the Save for Web dialog box.

9 Click Save. In the Save Optimized As dialog box, navigate to the advps10lessons folder and double-click to select the site folder located inside.

10 In the File Name text field, type **index**. This page will be the initial start page for the test website.

11 In the Format drop-down menu, choose HTML and Images

12 Choose Other for Settings; the Output Settings dialog box appears. In this dialog box you can set your preferences for how you want Photoshop to create your code. Click the Next button on the right to move to the Slices settings.

13 In the Slices settings, click the Generate CSS radio button. You can leave the CSS settings at their default. Click OK.

You can export your code as a table or in CSS.

14 Make sure All Slices is selected in the Slices drop-down menu and click Save.

15 Open your browser and choose File > Open and navigate to **index.html** to view your menu.

Self study

Now that you have experienced resizing and optimizing an image for the Web, go through the steps on your own to optimize the image of the children making smoothies (image **advps1008.jpg**, located in your advps10lessons folder). In its final form, the image should maintain as much quality as possible and be 225 pixels wide and 150 pixels high.

Review

Questions

1 Which is the more important factor to pay attention to when resizing a web image: pixel size or resolution?

2 What is the best format for an *animated* graphic that contains many gradients?

3 What format can you save in that allows you to fade an image and see through to the objects underneath it on a web page?

Answers

1 Pixel size is more important for web images (resolution is more important for printed output).

2 The GIF format is currently the *only* format that supports animation.

3 The PNG-24 format allows you save an image with varying levels of transparency.

Lesson 11

What you'll learn in this lesson:

- Creating an action
- Creating a droplet
- Processing batch actions
- Using Photomerge

Zipping it up with Automation Tools

In this lesson, you'll learn to use the automation tools to save you time and frustration, use the Actions panel, and turn your actions into Droplets for quick batch actions. You will also discover how to use other batch tools.

Starting up

Before starting, make sure that your tools and panels are consistent by resetting your preferences. See "Resetting Adobe Photoshop CC preferences" in the Starting up section of this book. You will work with several files from the advps11lessons folder in this lesson. Make sure that you have loaded the advpslessons folder onto your hard drive from the supplied DVD. For more information, see "Loading lesson files" in the Starting up section of this book.

See Lesson 11 in action!

Use the accompanying video to gain a better understanding of how to use some of the features shown in this lesson. You can find the video tutorial for this lesson on the included DVD.

What is an action?

An action allows you to record a set or sequence of steps in Photoshop. Essentially, an action is a script that records the steps, settings, and order in which you work in Photoshop. You can edit, tweak, and batch your recorded actions.

Creating a simple action

In this part of the lesson, you will create a simple action and then apply it to multiple images. To create an action, use the Actions panel.

1   Choose File > Open, navigate to the advps11lessons folder, and open the file named **advps1101.psd**; an image of a DJ's hands and a table appear, along with some text. In this first section, you will test an action preset, and then record your own action of you resizing and sharpening the image.

The original DJ image.

2   Choose File > Save As. When the Save As dialog box appears, type **advps1101_work** into the Name text field. Make sure that you are saving into the advps11lessons folder and that the format is set to Photoshop. Click Save.

3 Choose Window > Actions to open the Actions Panel. The Actions panel appears and includes a list of preset actions. You will use one of these actions to see how actions work. Select the Background layer in the Layers panel, so the Background will be the target of any action you select.

*A. Stop playing/recording. **B.** Begin recording. **C.** Play selection. **D.** Create new set. **E.** Create new action. **F.** Delete.*

4 Scroll down in the Actions panel and select the Gradient Map action, and then click the Play selection button (▶) at the bottom of the Actions panel.

Apply the Gradient Map Action.   *The results.*

In the next step, you will revert to save so you can test the action again, confirming each step as it occurs. This will give you an opportunity to see the types of functionality that can be saved in an action.

5 Choose File > Revert to revert the **advps1101_work.psd** file back to the last saved version.

6 In the Actions panel, notice that there is a Toggle dialog box on/off button (▣) to the left of the Gradient map action. Click the toggle button to turn on dialog boxes when the action is next run. If a warning appears, click OK.

Turn off or on dialog boxes with each step in an action.

7 Click the Play selection button again and note that a New Snapshot dialog box appears. The settings were already made for this action when it was originally recorded, so you can just click OK. Next, a New Layer dialog box appears followed by a Gradient Map dialog box. Continue clicking OK to see all the steps that were recorded in that action. As you can see, by turning on the Toggle dialog box, your action stops at each step to allow you to edit the settings before moving on.

8 Click the expansion arrow to the left of the Gradient Map action to see the steps in a list.

See all the steps in the action.

9 Choose File > Save. Keep this file open for the next part of the lesson.

Creating your own action

In this next exercise, you will record a sequence of steps and save them as an action. Your sequence of steps will apply some effects to your text layer.

1   With the **advps1101_work** file still open, select the Get the Beat layer. You will now create a new set, or folder, in which to save the actions you create.

2   Click the Create new set icon (▢) located at the bottom of the Actions panel; a New Set dialog box appears.

3   In the Name text field, type **My Actions**, and then click OK. A folder appears at the bottom of the list of actions.

4   Click the Create new action button (▣) at the bottom of the Actions panel; when the New Action dialog box appears, type **My Type Effect**.

5   For color, select Red. You won't see this color until later in the lesson when the view of the Actions panel is changed. Click Record when you are done. A red circle in the Actions panel indicates that your steps are being recorded.

Start recording your own script.

Note that any steps that you make will be recorded in your script. Mouse movements and time are not recorded.

6   Confirm that you have the Get the Beat layer selected in the Layers panel. Click the Add a layer style button (*fx*) at the bottom of the Layers panel and select Stroke; the Layer Style dialog box appears with the settings selected for the Stroke effect.

The default width and color of black for the stroke are selected and previewed on the screen. You will change these settings while recording.

7   Click the box to the right of Color; the Color Picker appears. Move your cursor over the image area to see that you can click to sample a color for your stroke from anywhere in the image. For this exercise, a dark purple is selected; you can select a different color. After sampling a color, click OK to return to the Layer Style dialog box.

Sample a color from the image.

8   Type **10** into the Stroke size and change the Blending mode to Darken.

9   Click the word Drop Shadow in the column on the left; the settings change to Drop Shadow options.

10 Enter **35** into the Size text field. Click the text in the image area and drag down to reposition the drop shadow so it is beneath the text. Click OK.

11 Choose File > Save. Keep the file open for the next part of the lesson.

Next, you will reduce the image in size and save it for the Web.

Adding an Image Size and a Save action

In this next part, you will record Image size and Save for the Web.

1   With the **advps1101_work** file still open, choose Image > Image Size; the Image Size dialog box appears.

2   Make sure that the units are set to pixels.

3 Enter **500** into the Width text field and choose Bicubic Sharper (reduction) from the Resample drop-down menu. This method maintains more details in your image when it is reduced. Click OK.

Change the Width to 500 pixels.

4 Choose File > Save for Web; the Save for Web dialog box appears. You will select a preset for this image.

5 From the Preset drop-down menu in the upper-right, select PNG-24 and click Save.

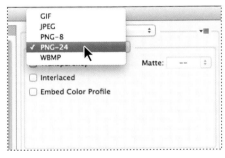

Choose to save the images using the PNG-24 preset.

6 In the Save Optimized As dialog box, type the name **dj01** and make sure that you are saving into the advps11lessons folder. Click Save.

7 Click the Stop recording button (■) in the Layers panel. Your action has been recorded. You will now test by using it on a different image file.

8 Choose File > Save, and then File > Close to close this file.

Playing your action

In this next section, you will play your action in another image file.

1 Choose File > Open and select the file named **advps1102.psd** located in your advps11lessons folder. An image of another DJ appears. You will run the action one time to see how saving a file within an action is resolved, and will then edit your action to complete the task correctly.

2 In the **advps1102.psd** file, make sure that the Busy Beat text layer is selected.

3 From the Actions panel, select My Text Effect and then click the Play selection button (▶) at the bottom of the Layers panel.

The text layer has the correct effect applied, the file is reduced to 500 pixels, and it is saved as a PNG file. The problem with this set of actions is that the script also recorded the name you used for the PNG file that you saved in the previous exercise. By running the My Type Effect Action, you replaced your initial image with this second image. In a production scenario, it would not be advantageous to run fifty images through an action to be left with only the last image. In the next part of this lesson, you will learn how to edit steps in a script.

4 Choose File > Revert to revert the file back to the original file.

5 Choose View > Fit on Screen. Keep the file open for the next part of the lesson.

Editing your script to change settings

In the next part, you will force the script to stop at the export stage so you can customize the file name.

1 Expand the My Text Effect action in the Actions panel and click the Toggle dialog box off/on button to the left of the Export step.

Click the Toggle dialog box off/on button.

2 Click the Play selection button and note that the Save for Web dialog box appears at the end and is waiting for you to click Save. By turning on a dialog box, you can essentially stop the script so you can customize it dynamically.

3 Click Cancel to close the Save for Web dialog box.

You can also skip a step in an action, as the following steps will show.

Later in this lesson, you will learn a different method for handling file names when working with batches of files.

4 Choose File > Revert to go back to the original file again.

5 Click the checkmark to the far left of the Export step and play the action again. The checkmark disappears and red warning checkmarks appear to the left of some of the previous steps. The red check mark indicates that some of the steps in the action are now disabled. This time, notice that the Save for Web step is ignored.

6 In the expanded set of the My Text Effect action, check the box to the left of the Export step so that it plays this step.

7 Turn off the Toggle dialog box icon to the left of Export so the Save for Web dialog box does not appear when the script is run next.

8 Choose File > Close to close the image file; do not save this file. Your action is saved even if you do not save the image file.

Creating a Droplet

In this next part, you will take an existing Action and convert it into a Droplet. A Droplet is essentially an application that can run batches of your selected action.

1 Make sure that you still have the My Type Effect Action selected in the Actions panel.

2 Choose File > Automate > Create Droplet; the Create Droplet dialog box appears.

3 Click the Save Droplet in section; in the Save As dialog box that appears, navigate to your Desktop.

4 Type **My Text Effect Droplet** into the Name text field, and then click Save.

Since you had the My Type Layers action selected when choosing the Create Droplet function, it should already be listed as the action. Note that you can suppress other warnings in the Play section as well. For this example, you will leave all settings in the Play section as they are.

5 In the Destination drop-down menu, choose Folder and then click the Choose button. Navigate to the advps11lessons folder and select the folder named **Completed_Files**. Click OK.

If you look further in the Destination folder, you will see that a script for automatically naming your file with an extension is already part of the Droplet script. Adding this batch renaming to the script prevents you from running multiple files through your action and having them override each other with an identical name.

Choose to save your action as droplet.

6 Click OK. If you look at the Desktop, you should see your Droplet.

You will now use the droplet to run your action on several images.

Using a Droplet

In this next section, you will take several files and apply the action using the Droplet. The Droplet allows you to drag files or even entire folders to run batch actions.

1 Using your directory system, locate the folder **Batch_Files** within your advps11lessons folder.

2 Click and drag the **Batch_Files** folder on top of My Text Effect Droplet. The images are opened and the script is run on each file. The files are then saved into the **Completed_Files** folder.

3   If you have any files open in Photoshop from this lesson, choose File > Close to close
them now.

*If you change your script after making into a Droplet, you will need to choose Automate >
Create Droplet and run through the steps again.*

Running a Batch action from within Photoshop

Instead of creating a Droplet, you can run a batch action directly from the Automate menu
item. To do this, you would select File > Automate > Batch. This feature also adds the
capability to change the file name and add extensions into the action.

The Batch action dialog box is similar to the Droplet's dialog box.

Using the Panorama feature in Photoshop

In this next section, you will run the Panorama Action that is available in the Automate section of Photoshop CC. You can use Photomerge to take three separate images and automatically combine them into one seamless image. Keep in mind that there must be an overlap between the images or an error will occur.

1 Choose File > Automate > Photomerge. The Photomerge dialog box appears.

You will now select three files to merge together.

2 Leave Use set at Files and click the Browse button.

3 In the Open dialog box, navigate to the advps11lessons folder and select the **advps1106a.psd** file. Shift+click the **advps1106b.psd** file and the **advps1106c.psd** file. Click Open. You are returned to the Photomerge dialog box.

4 Leave the Layout set to Auto and make sure that only Blend Images Together is checked at the bottom. Click OK. The action starts to run on your set of image files.

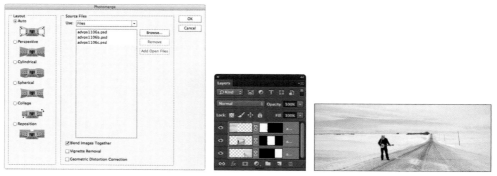

Choose to merge three files together.   Layers are positioned   The result.
                                          and masked.

5 Choose File > Save. In the Name text field, type **advps06_work.psd**. Make sure you save the file into the advps11lessons folder and that it remains in the Photoshop format. Click Save.

6 Choose File > Close.

Creating your own keyboard shortcuts

In this next section, you will learn to easily create your own shortcuts using the Actions panel. This is quite helpful for menu items that you might want to access quickly that don't have keyboard shortcuts. To discover how the process works, you will create an Action to open the Place menu item.

1 Make sure that you can see your Actions panel. If it is not visible, choose Window > Actions now.

2 Select the Create new action button (◻) at the bottom of the Actions panel.

3 When the New Action dialog box appears, type **Place** into the Name text field; make sure you are saving into My Actions (the set you created earlier in the lesson).

4 For this action, you will use a keyboard shortcut. In this example, the F9 key was selected and the modifier key (Shift) was checked.

5 Assign the color of Orange, and then click Record.

You will not perform any steps, since that would add settings and other unnecessary information in your script.

Create an action for a keyboard shortcut.

6 From the Actions panel menu, select Insert Menu Item; the Insert Menu Item dialog box appears. It is simply waiting for you to select a menu item from the menu in the Photoshop UI.

Select Insert Menu Item.

7 Choose File > Place; it is recorded as the menu item.

8 Click OK in the Insert Menu Item dialog box.

9 Click the Stop recording button at the bottom of the Layers panel.

Using actions in Button mode

When using actions, you can create a highly effective dashboard of all your actions by changing the view to Button mode.

1   Make sure you can see your Actions panel and select Button Mode from the panel menu. The panel is now shown as colored buttons that you can directly click to run your action. There is no need for the Play selection button.

2   Detach the Actions panel by dragging it into the work area by its tab, then click and drag the bottom right side to elongate it and expose the buttons in a horizontal view. This way you can position it across the bottom for easier access.

Click and drag the right side of Action panel to extend it horizontally.

Self study

To help you truly understand the capabilities of actions, you can test some of the default actions and change settings. Here are some interesting steps to try:

1   Use the image named **advps1101.psd** and make sure that the Background is selected.

2   Restore the Actions panel to list view by turning off Button Mode in the Actions Panel menu.

3   Select Stars Trails from the Actions Panel menu and then turn off the Flatten Image step by clicking the checkmark at the far left.

4   Select the Stars Trails Rotation action, and then play the Action on the Background. Notice how you can create an interesting effect and still keep the other layers editable.

Keep only the actions that you want by deleting some of the default actions that you will never use. You can always choose reset if you want them back in the Panel menu. This way, when you change to Button mode, you only have your key actions visible.

Review

Questions

1   How do you make an action skip a step when playing?

2   What is at least one solution to the challenge of overwriting existing files when a file name is added to a save action?

3   What could be wrong if you receive an error when running the Photomerge action?

Answers

1   You can make an action skip a step by selecting the Toggle item on/off check mark to the left of the step.

2   To avoid overwriting existing files when a file name is added in an action, you can turn on the dialog box for the save or export step. This allows you to change the name before saving the file. You can also use a batch action in which you can include a File Naming script to change file names and add extensions to them.

3   An error can occur when running the Photomerge action when the images have no significant overlap in image data for Photoshop to match up.

What you'll learn in this lesson:

- Creating 3D objects
- Controlling object appearance with textures and lighting
- 3D scene management

Using Photoshop for 3D

In this lesson, you will be introduced to the 3D functionality included in Photoshop CC, using some of the basic tools and features needed to leverage 3D content in your image editing workflow.

Starting up

Before starting, make sure that your tools and panels are consistent by resetting your preferences. See "Resetting Adobe Photoshop CC preferences" in the Starting up section of this book. You will work with several files from the advps12lessons folder in this lesson. Make sure that you have loaded the advpslessons folder onto your hard drive from the supplied DVD. For more information, see "Loading lesson files" in the Starting up section of this book.

See Lesson 12 in action!

Use the accompanying video to gain a better understanding of how to use some of the features shown in this lesson. You can find the video tutorial for this lesson on the included DVD.

Creating 3D objects

One of the most common questions asked about 3D in Photoshop is how to create the 3D content. Complex models, also called "meshes", need to be created in other dedicated 3D modeling applications, such as Cinema4D, Autodesk Maya, or 3ds Max. However, you can create simple 3D objects directly in Photoshop, and use 2D layers to create 3D meshes.

3D Hardware

Photoshop needs OpenGL enabled for many of the features covered here, so make sure your computer meets the minimum system requirements and that your graphics card (GPU) is supported. Most importantly, with Photoshop CC your graphics card must have a minimum of 512MB VRAM to support GPU acceleration.

Creating primitives

In this part of the lesson, you will create simple primitive objects using the Mesh From Preset feature in Photoshop. This will allow you to insert predefined 3D objects into your Photoshop document.

1   Choose File > New and then select the Web preset, which sets the canvas size to 800 pixels by 600 pixels and the resolution to 72 pixels per inch. The canvas should be small when you work with the 3D files so your rendering times can be kept down later in the process. Click OK. You will now create a layer to hold your 3D content.

2   If you do not see your Layers panel, choose Windows > Layers now. In the Layers panel, press and hold the Alt (Windows) or Option (Mac OS) key, and then click the Create a new layer button (▣). When the New Layer dialog box appears, type **3D Objects** for the name and click OK. A new layer is created.

3 Choose Window > Workspace > 3D. You now see the Properties panel on the right and the 3D panel directly below that.

Create a new 3D object from a set of predefined meshes.

4 In the 3D panel, you can see a Create New 3D Object section and the source set to the selected layers. In this case, the Background layer is selected by default, so the Background layer will be converted to a 3D layer when you create your object.

5 Choose the Mesh from Preset option and choose Sphere from the drop-down menu. Then click the Create button.

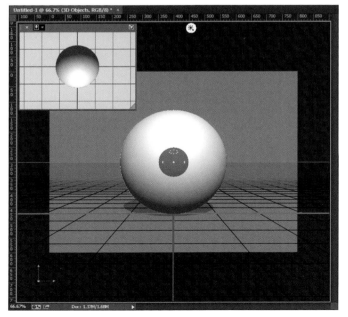

A new spherical 3D object has been created in Photoshop.

6 Choose File > Save. In the Save As dialog box, type **Photoshop3D** into the File Name text field and then verify that the format is Photoshop (.PSD). Make sure that your destination folder is advps12lessons folder, and then click Save.

At this point, you have created a 3D object in Photoshop quickly and easily, but as you can see, there are only a limited number of available presets for these meshes. Next, you will find out how to make more customizable 3D content.

Extruding paths

You can use 2D Photoshop elements, including layers, paths, and selections, to create customized 3D objects. In this part of the lesson, you will use the Custom Shape Tool to create a path and extrude that into a 3D object. To this end, you will make a new layer for your next 3D object.

1 In the Layers panel, Alt/Option+click the Create a new layer button (■), type **Fleur-De-Lis** into the Name text field, and click OK.

2 Select the Custom Shape tool (✿) from the Tools panel. Make sure that the tool is set to "Path" in the Options panel so the result of this tool will be a path. Choose the Fleur-De-Lis shape from the default shapes palette.

Using the Custom Shape Tool to create a path in the shape of a fleur-de-lis.

3 Click and drag to draw the path anywhere on your new layer. You can press and hold the Shift key to constrain the proportions; try to make the new shape roughly the same size as the sphere. When you release, the new path is selected.

4 Choose 3D > New 3D Extrusion from Selected Path to convert this path into a customizable 3D object. The path is now a 3D object and your layer has been converted to a 3D layer. Let's make this 3D object a bit more ornate.

5 By default, the 3D scene properties are shown when a new 3D layer is created. Click the new 3D Fleur-De-Lis object, and notice that the object name in the 3D panel is the same as the layer name we assigned it previously. As the selection changes to the Fleur-De-Lis, the Properties panel reveals new settings that control the 3D features of our new extruded object.

6   Selecting the Shape Preset thumbnail in the Properties panel, and then select the Inflate shape preset. You can experiment with other presets if you wish.

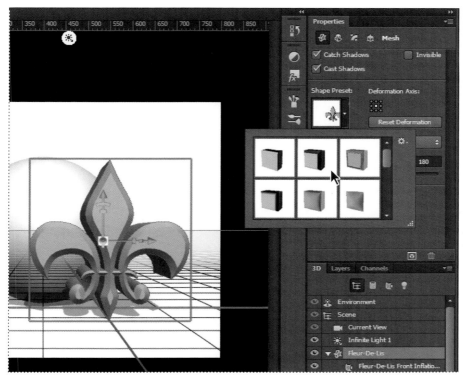

Applying a bevel to an extruded 3D object.

At this point, you have two different 3D objects on two different layers. These objects are in their own scene and have their own default lighting and camera, and they don't interact with each other. That means that the lighting from your Fleur-De-Lis layer isn't sharing the same lighting highlights or casting shadows onto the sphere, because they are on different layers and in different 3D scenes. You'll merge these two layers so these objects share the same 3D space.

7   Go to the Layers panel and select the Fleur-De-Lis layer. Make sure that no other layers are selected. Click the Layers panel menu and select Merge Down to combine this layer with the 3D Objects layer. You might see your objects shift position slightly. Now both of your objects are on the same 3D layer and will share lighting and shadows.

8   If you need to reposition the Fleur-De-Lis object select the Fleur-De-Lis Layer in the 3D panel, position your cursor over the Fleur-De-Lis object and then click and drag down. You will see a Tooltip indication that you are Moving along the Z axis.

9   Choose File > Save and save this file. Keep the file open for the next part of this lesson.

Extruding 3D text

You can create great-looking 3D text from traditional 2D text in Photoshop, and you can combine that text with other 3D objects, too.

1 Select the Horizontal Type tool (T) from the Tools panel and click anywhere in the image area to type **Extruded Text**. Using the Set the font family drop-down menu, in the Options panel, select a typeface that you would like to use. Note that typefaces with thicker strokes generally work better for extruded text.

2 With the newly created text layer selected, choose 3D > New 3D Extrusion from Selected Layer; the text layer becomes a new 3D layer and the 3D panel has been activated. Now you will combine your new 3D text with our other layer containing 3D objects.

3 In the Layers panel, select the Extruded Text layer and the 3D Objects layer. Choose 3D > Merge 3D Layers to combine all 3D objects into one layer and one scene.

4 Make sure that both the Properties and the 3D panels are visible, and then click the 3D text in your scene. Notice how the related object is highlighted in the 3D panel and the options change in the Properties panel. Now let's edit our 3D text by making sure it is selected and then clicking Edit Source in the Properties panel.

5 A new document titled Extruded Text.psb opens. This is a temporary file that contains the source content of your 3D layer before it was extruded. Edit the text using the Text tool, changing the text from Extruded Text to **Fleur-De-Lis**.

6   Choose Create Warped Text (工)from the Options panel to warp the 2D text. From the Warp Text dialog box, choose the Arc style option and set the Bend amount to **70%** and the Vertical Distortion to **-10%**. Click OK, and then click and drag to reposition your text.

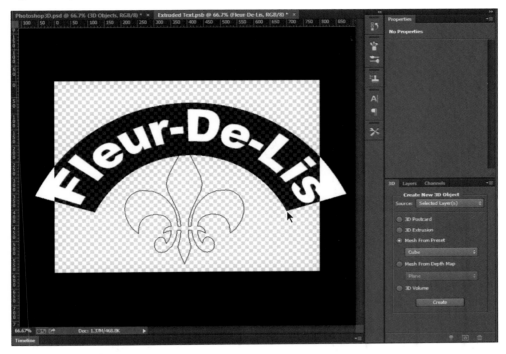

You can edit 3D text objects.

7   Choose File > Save and then close this temporary PSB file. You should see your 3D text updated in your scene.

Viewing and transforming 3D objects

Now that you have created several 3D objects using different techniques in Photoshop, you'll look at how to arrange these in 3D space. Similar to the transformations you use on 2D elements, you have the ability to move, rotate, and scale objects, but in three dimensions. You also now have to consider the viewing angle and distance when creating a composition, which can be defined by the current view or cameras in your scene.

Working with 3D camera tools

You will now have the opportunity to experiment with the 3D camera tools to change your current view. In Photoshop CC, the camera tools are shown when the Move tool (✛) is active and you have a 3D layer selected. The 3D camera tools allow you to quickly change your viewing angle or viewing distance in the scene. Now you will take your current view of the scene and pull back to reveal all the objects and center them.

1 Select the Move tool (✛) from the Tools panel. You will see the 3D camera tools to the right in the Options panel. Make sure the 3D panel is visible and click the Current View element. Note that the information displayed in the Properties panel has changed to that of a 3D Camera.

2 The field of view, or FOV, of the camera approximates the view from a telephoto lens (higher values) to a wide–angle lens (lower values). Click Scale the 3D Object (🔲) in the Options panel and then click and drag vertically in the 3D scene. Note the value for FOV updates as you release the mouse button.

3 With a focal length defined, you will position the camera to fit all of the elements in the scene. With the Move tool active, click the Slide the 3D Object button (🔲) and click and drag vertically in the scene. This moves your camera towards and away from the objects as you drag down and up, respectively. You can also drag left and right to position the camera horizontally.

4 Select Drag the 3D Object (🔲) from the Options panel. Because you have the Current View selected in the 3D panel, dragging in the scene horizontally will pan the camera to the left or right, and dragging vertically will move your viewpoint up or down.

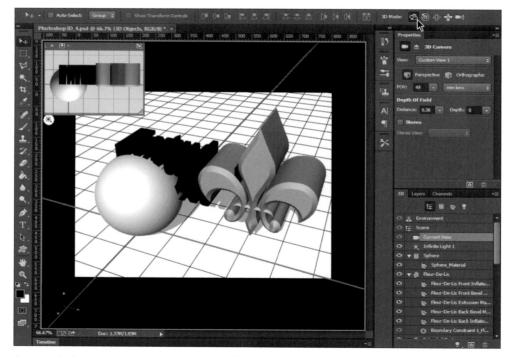

Camera tools allow you to change the viewing angle and distance as you work in your scene.

5   Choose Rotate the 3D Object (⬢) from the Options panel and click and drag in the scene to rotate the viewing angle of the current view. Note that the location of your viewpoint isn't changing, but the orientation or angle of your view is changing. Rotate the viewing angle so you can see some of the depth of the extruded text and shapes.

6   For controlling the tilt angle of the camera, choose Roll the 3D Object and click and drag in the scene to adjust the rotation of the camera on its viewing axis.

7   Use all of the 3D camera tools to create a view that shows all of your objects in the 3D scene. Save this view as a new camera by selecting the View drop-down menu in the Properties panel and choosing Save. Give the new 3D view the name **Perspective view – All Objects**. This view is added at the very bottom of the 3D panel. Clicking the saved view returns the camera to this exact position and rotation.

Next, you will position these objects relative to each other.

Using the 3D object tools

You have successfully changed your viewing angle by changing the position and rotation of your current view. Now you will change the position, rotation, and scale of the various objects in your scene. One feature that is particularly helpful when transforming objects is the secondary window that appears in the upper left corner when a 3D layer is selected. This secondary window allows you to see your scene from multiple viewing angles simultaneously. Another important tool for transforming objects is the 3D Axis, and you will use this tool to move, rotate, and scale individual objects.

1 With the Move tool (✛) active in the Tools panel, select the Sphere object that you created. You can click the sphere on the canvas or you can click the Sphere element in the 3D panel. The Sphere becomes highlighted and has a bounding box drawn around it with a red, green, and blue 3D Axis at the center of the object. If you don't see this, turn on the axis by choosing View > Show > 3D Selection.

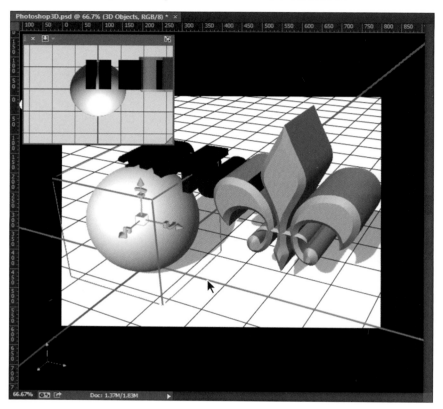

Use the 3D Axis to move, rotate, and scale individual objects.

2 Now you will change the position of your sphere using the 3D Axis. Move the cursor to the conical arrowheads at the end of the red axis. A tooltip appears to indicate this is the Move On X Axis. Click and drag to move your Sphere object in the X direction. Note that the 3D Secondary View updates and shows the sphere moving in a top view. Release the mouse button to stop moving the object.

3 It is difficult to see rotational changes in a perfectly spherical object, so you will change the selection to the Fleur-De-Lis object by clicking it. You now see the 3D Axis for the Sphere object disappear and a 3D Axis appear at the center of the Fleur-De-Lis object.

4 Hold the cursor over the arc segment on the green axis. A yellow circle appears, extending the arc segment. Click and drag to Rotate Around the Z Axis. Note that the angle of rotation appears while you rotate.

5   Press Ctrl+Z (Windows) or Command+Z (Mac OS) to undo the rotation you just made. Now hold the cursor over the white box at the center of the 3D Axis until the box changes to yellow. Click and drag to change the scale of the Fleur-De-Lis object. This is a uniform scale transformation, which means that the object is being scaled the same amount in each direction. Scale the Fleur-De-Lis object so it is approximately the same size as the Sphere object.

6   Now you will apply a non-uniform scale to the Sphere object. Click the Sphere object and hold the cursor over the blue box on the 3D Axis. If the selection is not clearly visible, change the viewing angle or distance by clicking Current View in the 3D panel and then using the Camera tools to change your view orientation. With the Sphere object selected, click and drag the box on the blue axis to Scale Along Z Axis. Reduce the scale in the Z Axis to approximately 50%, and note the change in appearance in the 3D Secondary View.

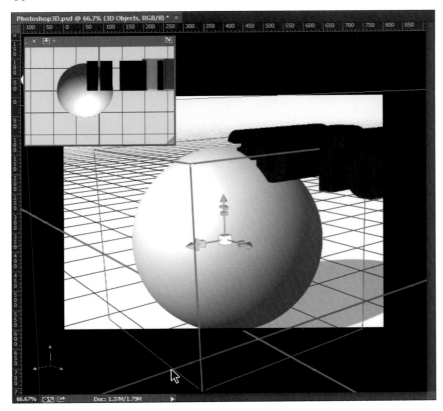

Objects can be scaled in only one direction.

7   Select the Fleur-De-Lis and use the Move, Rotate, and Scale tools in the 3D Axis to position the Fleur-De-Lis in front of the Sphere so it overlaps the sphere in 3D space. Scale the Fleur-De-Lis to fit inside the sphere so it appears to be extending out from the sphere.

8   Select the Extruded Text object and position it above the sphere and Fleur-De-Lis objects. Adjust the uniform scale as needed to size the text to surround the sphere.

9   Go back to your original viewing angle by clicking the Perspective View – All Objects at the bottom of the 3D panel. This is the camera view you saved previously.

At this point, you have created several 3D objects and manipulated them in 3D space to create a complete design composition. Next, you'll look at how to change the appearance of these 3D objects and render them out as final 2D images.

Object appearances

Most of the 3D work that you do using Photoshop will eventually be rendered out as 2D pixels, so you need to make sure the appearance of your objects is appealing. Every 3D object in Photoshop has one or more materials assigned to it to define the appearance of its surfaces, from the color to how shiny or bumpy it is. You should note that the appearance of a material in the final image is also a function of the mesh surface and the lighting in the scene, so you should refine materials and lighting at the same time. Before you change any of the materials in this lesson, you'll add more dramatic lighting.

Lighting

By default, your 3D layer has an Infinite Light assigned to it, so you have some light in the scene to view your objects. This light simulates light coming from all directions and helps to avoid having very dark areas in your scene. If you turn off this light, you don't have highlights and shadows to define your models' surfaces.

1   In the 3D panel, select Infinite Light 1 and note the changes to the information in the Properties panel. With the light selected, you can see options to adjust the color of the light, the brightness or intensity, and whether this light casts shadows. If the light does cast shadows, you can see options to indicate how soft the edges of those shadows are.

2   Adjust the intensity down to approximately 50%. You will reduce this brightness since you will add another light to the scene. Turn off shadows for this light, since you will use a Spot Light to create shadows.

3   At the bottom of the 3D panel, select the Light button (◪) and add a New Spot Light to the scene.

4   The new spotlight appears. This is a light that emits rays in a conical shape in one direction. Use the 3D Axis tool to move the light around the scene. As you do, notice that the shadows cast by the objects change. If the light is no longer illuminating your objects, click the Point at origin (▣) button at the bottom of the Properties panel to direct it back at the origin.

5 In the Properties panel, set the Shadow softness to approximately 50%.

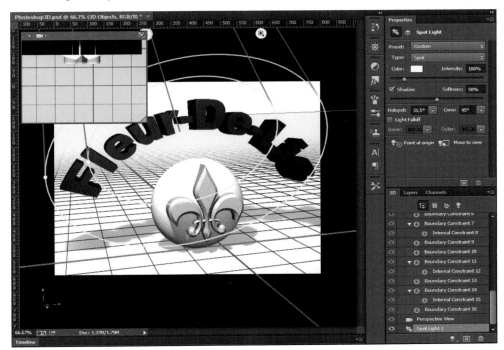

Spot Lights emit light in a cone-shaped pattern in a specific direction.

At this point, you have two lights in your scene. The Infinite Light provides general illumination, while the Spot Light, or your key light, provides the dramatic highlights and shadows for this image.

Materials

With your lighting set up, you can now make changes to the materials and see how they affect the resulting image. You will assign a gray metallic material to the Sphere object, a gold metallic material to the Fleur-De-Lis, and a green plastic material to the Extruded Text object.

1 Select the Sphere object in the scene. Notice that in the 3D panel, there is a material associated with this object called Sphere_Material. Click Sphere_Material to view the material parameters in the Properties panel.

2 Click the Diffuse color swatch in the Properties panel. Change the Diffuse color to 50% gray in the B (Brightness) field, and then press Enter or Return. This is the color of the object where light directly hits the surface.

3   Click the Specular color swatch in the Properties panel. Change the Specular color to 30% gray. Specular color is the color of the object where highlights are visible on the surface. This is typically the same hue as the Diffuse Color, but you can adjust lightness to make the highlights stronger or weaker.

4   Set the Shine value to **60%** in the Properties panel. Higher shine values represent more polished surfaces with smaller highlights.

5   Set the Reflection value to **40%** in the Properties panel. This controls the intensity of the reflections seen in the surface.

6   At the bottom of the 3D panel, click the Render button. Photoshop starts to calculate precise lighting, shadows, and reflections for your scene. This can be very time consuming, but you should be able to quickly see the reflection of the text appear in the surface of the sphere. You can wait for the render to complete or you can press Esc to cancel and keep working. The rendered image is what will be displayed for this 3D layer when you are finished.

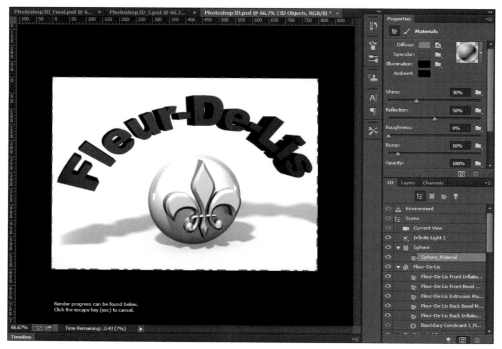

Rendering the scene shows refined shadows and reflections.

Your Sphere object has only one material for the entire surface of the object. Your extruded objects can have multiple materials, allowing for different materials to be assigned to the front and rear faces, bevels, and sides of the extrusion. You will leverage a library of existing materials to create gold metallic material for the Fleur-De-Lis.

1   Select the Fleur-De-Lis object in the scene. In the 3D panel, the Fleur-De-Lis object is highlighted with several materials listed below. Choose the first of these materials, Fleur-De-Lis Front Inflation Material, and view the material parameters in the Properties panel.

2   In the Properties panel, click the material preview to view a pop-up panel of available material presets. Scroll down and select Metal Gold. This assigns the Metal Gold material preset to the front face of the Fleur-De-Lis extrusion.

3   In the 3D panel, Ctrl+click (Windows) or Command+click (Mac OS) the other materials listed under the Fleur-De-Lis object, so all the materials are selected for this object. Do not select the Boundary Constraints. In the Properties panel, set them all to the Metal Gold preset. All surfaces of the Fleur-De-Lis object should now have reflective gold surfaces.

Material presets contain samples for metals, plastics, glass, and more.

4   Click the Render button at the bottom of the 3D panel to view the appearance of the newly applied materials.

Changing the properties of the extruded text

You will now make additional changes to the extruded text.

1   Select the Extruded Text object from the 3D panel.

2   Select all the materials listed below the Extruded Text object. Click the first material and then Shift+click the last material. All five materials for this object are now selected and highlighted.

3   Click the material preview in the Properties panel. Choose the Plastic Glossy (Blue) material to assign this new material to the Extruded Text object.

4   Because all the materials are selected, any changes you make in the Properties panel will affect all the faces of the Extruded Text object. Click the Diffuse color swatch in the Properties panel. Change the hue from blue to green (R:**0** G:**128** B:**0**) and click OK.

5   Now you will save your new material for future use. Click the material preview in the Properties panel to bring up the material preset pop-up and choose New Material from the panel menu. Type **My Glossy Green Plastic** in the Name text field for your new material.

6   Click the Render button (▣) at the bottom of the 3D panel to render out your scene for web, print, or animation.

7   When the render is complete, choose File > Save or press Ctrl+S (Windows) or Command+S (Mac OS) to save the document.

Rendering

Rendering is the process of generating a 2D image based on the 3D scene you have defined. It is roughly equivalent to taking a photograph of a real-world scene. Photoshop is projecting the 3D scene onto a 2D plane and calculating the pixels that need to be displayed. Photoshop uses raytracing and other CPU-intensive calculations, so your computer might become slow to respond while rendering, even with a multi-core processor. Render times can be lengthy and are typically based on the complexity of your scene, including the detail in your 3D objects, the number of lights, and the reflectivity or transparency of the materials you use. Rendering is also heavily dependent upon the canvas size.

Once a render is complete, the layer will display the 3D scene elements when selected, and the final rendered image when not selected.

Textures and painting

Textures are a natural way to add detail to 3D objects, and Photoshop has some great tools for using images to create patterns on the surface of various objects. Textures can be used to change the color of an object's surface, but also to control the level of reflectivity, transparency, or even surface bumpiness. You can add texture to any of the different settings for a given material.

Adding texture to a 3D object

You will create a new image to use as a texture for the Sphere object in your scene.

1   Select the Sphere_Material listed under the Sphere object in the 3D panel.

2   Click the folder icon to access the texture map menu for the Bump setting in the Properties panel. Choose New Texture, and in the New dialog box, set both the Width and Height to **512** pixels. Click OK.

Square textures

Textures should be square images with a pixel size that is a power of 2. This allows for easier scaling of the textures as the object travels into the distance and becomes smaller. For this exercise, you will create textures at 512×512 pixels, but you can create textures at 256×256 pixels, 1024×1024 pixels, or another smaller or larger size.

---

3   Click the folder icon to access the texture map menu for the Bump setting again, this time clicking Edit Texture. This brings up your texture in a new window, Sphere_Material-Bump.psb. Just as with the 2D text before, the texture information is stored in a temporary PSB file while you edit it.

4   At this point, you can paint directly on the texture, but you will generate a pattern quickly using Filters. Select Filter > Render > Clouds to create some clouds. To make these clouds more intense, choose Filter > Render > Difference Clouds. Now press Ctrl+F (Windows) or Command+F (Mac OS) several times to reapply that Difference Clouds filter.

5   Press Ctrl+S (Windows) or Command+S (Mac OS) to save the texture, and then close this file. The 3D scene is now visible and there is a faint bumpiness on the surface of the Sphere object.

6 Change the Bump setting in the Properties panel to 20% to make the Bump texture more prominent.

Textures can be applied to add more visual detail to 3D objects.

Painting a 3D object

You can also use the Brush tool (✐) in the Tools panel to paint onto any 3D object that has a defined texture. In this example, you will paint directly on the reflectivity texture for the Sphere object, making some parts of the surface less reflective than others.

1 Select the Sphere_Material listed under the Sphere object in the 3D panel.

2 Choose the texture map menu for the Reflection setting in the Properties panel. Choose New Texture, and in the New dialog box, set the width and height to **512** pixels. Click OK.

3 Click 3D > Paint on Target Texture > Reflectivity. This will assign any painted colors to the reflectivity textures for the objects.

4 Select the Brush tool (✐) in the Tools panel, right-click the canvas to open the Brush context menu, and change your brush settings. Change the brush size to **50** pixels and the hardness to **0** (zero).

5 Paint directly on the Sphere object. Note that the intensity of the reflections is reduced where you are painting. Use the Camera tools to change your viewing angle and paint the backside of the object.

6   To remove the painted texture, select the texture map menu for the Reflection setting in the Properties panel and click Remove Texture. The texture is deleted.

Using Photoshop 3D in production workflows

In this lesson, you have been introduced to the basic 3D functionality in Photoshop CC. While you created 3D objects directly in Photoshop from preset meshes and 2D layers, there is an opportunity to leverage more advanced 3D meshes from other applications. Photoshop CC can import and export a variety of 3D file formats.

Working with custom meshes

You can create a new 3D layer from an externally generated file by choosing 3D > New 3D Layer from File and then choosing the file in the Open dialog box. You can export similar file formats by right-clicking a 3D layer and selecting Export 3D Layer. Some of the file formats available for import and export are:

- **Collada files** (.dae file extension) use an open standard XML file format that you can use in a wide variety of 3D applications and game engines. Collada files can contain information on meshes, texture (UV) coordinates, materials, and even animation.

- **Stereolithography files** (.stl extension) are used in 3D printing, and can be generated from computer-aided design (CAD) models. These files don't support materials, texture coordinates, or animation.

- **WavefrontOBJ files** (.obj extension) are another file format that supports mesh topology, texture coordinates, and support for materials and texture maps when an accompanying .mtl file is provided.

Working with models imported from external 3D applications allows you to render 3D objects that are very complex and customized, and can save you a lot of time in production. For example, if STL files were created to 3D-print a prototype for a new product, you could import that same STL file into Photoshop and use it to render a 2D image of the product. In Photoshop, you could then adjust the materials and lighting as needed.

Downloading external 3D content

Just as 2D design has stock photography, 3D design has resources available to buy 3D content from third-party providers. From meshes to textures to customized lighting setups, there are many resources available online when looking for 3D assets. Some include:

http://www.photoshop.com/products/photoshop/3d

http://www.turbosquid.com/photoshop-3d

http://archive3d.net/

When browsing for 3D content online, remember to look for assets that are available in the file formats that Photoshop can import. There is a wide variety of 3D assets available online, including animals, electronics, buildings and furnishings, vehicles, human characters, and much more. These assets and Photoshop's 3D capabilities make it easier than ever to bring 3D into your image editing workflows.

Self study

One of the typical end uses of 3D content is to composite a rendered image into an existing image, making it appear as though your 3D model is part of the scene shown in the original image. The challenges to making a convincing composite are numerous, but much of the effort is spent trying to match 3D lights and shadows to the lighting shown in the image. Try taking a 3D object and compositing it into a background image, and see how seamlessly you can blend the two images.

Review

Questions

1   What are some of the preset mesh objects available in Photoshop CC?

2   What transformations can be made on an object using the 3D Axis?

3   What is rendering and why is it important for the 3D process?

Answers

1   Preset mesh objects include a cone, cube, cylinder, donut, hat, pyramid, ring, soda, sphere, and wine bottle.

2   The 3D Axis can be used to change an object's position, rotation, and scale. Position and rotation changes can be made along and around a specific axis, respectively. Scale can be adjusted either uniformly or along a specific axis.

3   Rendering is the process of generating a 2D image based on 3D scene elements. The final rendered image shows objects and their shadows at their highest quality. This image can then be used as an asset in any associated print, web, or video project.

Index

A

Accept and Go to Conflict button, 18
action(s)
    batch, 289
    in Button mode, 292
    creating, 283–284
    definition of, 280
    Droplet, 287–289
    editing script to change settings,
        286–287
    Image size added to, 284–285
    Panorama, 290
    playing, 286
    Save for the Web, 284–285
    simple, 280–282
Actions panel, 281, 291
Adaptive Wide Angle filter, 183–186
Add layer mask button, 55, 71, 159, 222
Add layer mask icon, 155, 181, 186
Add layer style button, 207, 228, 283
adding
    adjustment layer, 151–154
    features to images, 187–188
    Image size to action, 284–285
    images to composition, 176–179
    lighting effects, 208–213
    vector text, 224–228
adjusting
    Blending of filter, 142
    lighting, 210–211
adjustment layer
    adding, 151–154
    blending using, 192–193

retouching use of, 151–154
adjustment layer button, 65, 134, 153,
    160
Adobe Bridge
    automation tools, 51–53
    changing view of, 35–36
    color settings, 123
    Favorites, 40–41
    file browser use of, 34
    files
        batch renaming of, 51–53
        loading into Photoshop layers,
            55–56
        searching for, 48–50
    folders, 37–47
        Favorite, 40–41
        managing, 38
        stacking, 42
    Image Processor, 53–54
    images
        correcting, 56–57
        opening, 46
        stacking, 42
    keywords
        metadata, 45–46
        searching for files using, 48–50
    locked files, 44
    metadata
        creating, 42–45
        keywords, 45–46
        locating, 42–45
        template, creating, 47–48
    reasons for using, 34

searching for files
  Filter panel, 50–52
  by name or keyword, 48–50
workspaces, 37
Adobe Flash Player, 7
Adobe Illustrator, 235–236
aligning text, 26–27
Alt/Option key, 69, 93, 99
Ambience option, Properties panel, 211
anchor points, 87, 92
Angular Direction option, Oil Paint,
  201
animating GIF files, 258, 265–269
Apply button, 45
Artboard tool, 239
automation tools
  action. *See* action(s)
  Adobe Bridge, 51–53
Auto-Select, 212

B

Background layer, Smart Object
  created from, 104
backslash, 132
batch action, 289
Batch Rename dialog box, 52
batch renaming files, 51–53
black point, locating, 126–127
black Point eyedropper tool, 129
blending
  of features, 189, 192–193
  of filter, 142
Blending Mode drop-down menu, 151
bracket key, 135, 159

Bridge (Adobe)
  automation tools, 51–53
  changing view of, 35–36
  color settings, 123
  Favorites, 40–41
  file browser use of, 34
  files
    batch renaming of, 51–53
    loading into Photoshop layers,
      55–56
    searching for, 48–50
  folders, 37–47
    Favorite, 40–41
    managing, 38
    stacking, 42
  Image Processor, 53–54
  images
    correcting, 56–57
    opening, 46
    stacking, 42
  keywords
    metadata, 45–46
    searching for files using, 48–50
  locked files, 44
  metadata
    creating, 42–45
    keywords, 45–46
    locating, 42–45
    template, creating, 47–48
  reasons for using, 34
  searching for files
    Filter panel, 50–52
    by name or keyword, 48–50
  workspaces, 37

Bristle Detail option, Oil Paint, 201
browser window, 245
brush(es)
  custom, applying to path, 110
  editing, 109
  preset, defining, 108
Brush Preset Picker, 109, 162, 185
Brush tool, 109, 183, 190, 203
Burn tool, 166
Button mode, using actions in, 292

C

Camera Raw
  definition of, 204
  as Smart Filter, 204–207
Camera Raw dialog box, 56–57, 204
Cancel Current Crop Operation
      button, 248
centering of layer, 175
central control point, 180
chromatics, 119
chromatography, 119
Clack and drag in image button, 133
Cleanliness option, Oil Paint, 201
clipping group, 153, 171
clipping mask symbol, 192
clipping path, 112
Clone Stamp tool
  copying using, 185–187
  retouching using, 162–168
clone-stamping, 162–168
CMYK color mode, 121
Collada files, 313

color
  CMYK color mode, 121
  curve adjustments, 137
  curve corrections, 134–137
  histograms, 116–120
  midtones, adjusting, 130–131
  overview of, 116
  RGB color mode
    description of, 121
    highlight, 125, 128–129
    locating white and black point,
        126–127
    shadow, 125, 128–129
    working in, 122–125
  sharpening images, 138–142
color correction, 120–121
color gamut, 143
Color Lookup Tables, 194–196
Color Picker, 25, 214
Color Sampler tool, 127
color samplers, 127
Color Settings, 4
color settings
  CMYK color mode, 121
  RGB color mode
    description of, 121
    highlight, 125, 128–129
    locating white and black point,
        126–127
    shadow, 125, 128–129
    working in, 122–125
Color Settings dialog box, 4, 122
color table, GIF images, 261–264
color warnings, 4

colorimetry, 119

Colorize option, Properties panel, 210

compositions

Adaptive Wide Angle filter, 183–186

images added to

adding features to, 187–188

blending of features, 189, 192–193

place feature used for, 179–189

second image, 176–179

texture, 194

masking a layer, 181–183

removing features from, 190–195

Smart Filters, 174–176

Smart Objects, 174–179

Content-Aware, 146

copying

Clone Stamp tool for, 185–187

lesson files to hard drive, 5

.cr2, 204

Create a New Folder icon, 39

Create new brush icon, 109

Create new layer icon, 162

Create new set icon, 22

creating

actions, 283–284

compositions. *See* compositions

guides, 87–88

keyboard shortcuts, 17–21, 290–291

metadata, 42–45

paths, 87–88

3D objects, 296–301

Crop tool, 147, 248

.crw, 204

curve adjustments, 137

curve corrections, 134–137

Curves Adjustments panel, 125–126

Curves Properties panel, 131

custom meshes, 313

Custom Shape tool, 298

customizing

panels, 28–29

workspaces, 29–30

D

DCS 2.0 format, 112

Default Lasso tool, 66

default settings, 3–4

deleting

guides, 24

Smart Filter, 204

workspaces, 30

depth of field, 212–213

diagonal line segment, 92, 192

dialog boxes

Batch Rename, 52

Camera Raw, 56–57, 204

Color Settings, 4, 122

EPS Options, 112

Find, 49

Guides, Grids & Slices, 246

Image Processor, 53

Insert Menu Item, 291

Keyboard Shortcuts and Menus, 20–21

Layer Style, 228–232

Lens Correction, 169

New Layer, 185

New Snapshot, 282

New Workspace, 29

Preferences, 25, 246

Refine Edge, 74–75, 77

Save As, 112, 117, 147, 200
Save Path, 100
Spellchecker, 19
Threshold, 126–127
UnSharp Mask, 139, 249–250
Warped Text, 215
Direct Selection tool, 91
directional line, 90
dithering, 261
Dodge tool, 166
drag and drop technique, 176
drop shadow, 230–232
Droplet, 287–289
dynamic panning, 12
dynamic zooming, 12

E

Edge Detection, 77
editing
   brushes, 109
   paths, 91
   script to change settings, actions,
      286–287
Elliptical Marquee tool, 61
Embedded Profile Mismatch
      warning, 4
EPS format, 112
EPS Options dialog box, 112
Erase refinement tool, 75
Essentials button, 35
Exposure option, Properties panel, 210
Extensible Metadata Platform, 43
Extras
   grids, 25–27
   guides, 25–27

turning off and off, 28
extruded text, 310
Extruded Text layer, 300
Eyedropper tool, 127, 262

F

Favorites (Bridge), 35, 40–41
Favorites panel, 40–41
feather value, 148
feathering the mask, 72
files
   batch renaming, 51–53
   locked, 44
   Mac OS, 6
   searching for
      Filter panel, 50–52
      by name or keyword, 48–50
filter(s)
   Adaptive Wide Angle, 183–186
   blending of, adjusting, 142
   painting of, on image, 141
   Smart Filters
      Camera Raw as, 204–207
      compositions, 140, 174–176
      deleting, 204
      Oil Paint as, 200
      power of, 203
Filter (Bridge), 35
Filter panel, 50–52
Find dialog box, 49
Fit on Screen function, 11
Flash Player (Adobe), 7
Folders (Bridge), 35
Full Screen mode, 16

G

GIF format
  description of, 111
  images saved in. *See* GIF images
GIF images
  animating, 258, 265–269
  color table, 261–264
  compression algorithms for, 258
  description of, 258–259
  matte added to, 264–265
  optimizing, 260–261
Gloss option, Properties panel, 210
Gradient preset drop-down menu, 208
Gradient tool, 223, 271
Graphics Interchange Format, 111
gray value, 120, 124, 143
grids
  aligning text using, 26–27
  using, 25–26
guides
  aligning text using, 26–27
  creating, 87–88
  deleting, 24
  Pen tool for creating, 87–88
  using, 23–24
Guides, Grids & Slices dialog box, 246

H

Hand tool, 13, 212
hard drive
  copying lesson files to, 5
  copying video tutorials to, 7
Hexadecimal values, 263
"high-key" image, 118
highlights

defining, 128–129
locating white and black point,
    126–127
setting, 125
Histogram panel, 116–118
histograms, 116–120
HSL/Grayscale icon, 205
HTML, saving slicing as, 276
Hue, 205
hyperlinks, 274

I

Illustrator (Adobe), 235–236
image(s)
  adding to composition, 176–179
  adjusting the size of, 247–248
  balancing neutrals in, 131–134
  browser window size and, 245
  color correction of, 120–121
  correcting, 56–57
  curve adjustments, 137
  DCS 2.0 format, 112
  Edge Detection, 77
  EPS format, 112
  file format of, 250–261
  GIF. *See* GIF images
  "high-key," 118
  histograms, 116–120
  JPEG. *See* JPEG images
  opening, 46
  painting filter on, 141
  Pen tool use with, 95–100
  PNG, 111–112, 269–272
  previewing, 254–255
  resizing, 244–246

saving, for other applications, 111–113
sharpening of, 138–142
size, adjusting, 247–248
slicing, 273–277
stacking, 42
texture added to, 194
total pixel dimensions of, 244
Unsharp Mask filter applied to, 249–250
vignette added to, 168–170
Image Processor, 53–54
Image Processor dialog box, 53
Infinite, 209
Input values, 160
Insert Menu Item dialog box, 291
IPTC Core, 43

J

JPEG images
    choosing quality of, 251–253
    previewing, 254–255
    saving, 251
    saving settings, 257
    transparency effect in, 255–256

K

keyboard shortcuts
    creating, 17–21, 290–291
    Elliptical Marquee tool, 61
    navigational, 11
    saving, 20–21
    using, 19
Keyboard Shortcuts and Menus dialog
    box, 20–21
keywords
    metadata, 45–46

searching of files using, 48–50
Keywords (Bridge), 35

L

Lasso tool, 148
    alternating between, 67–71
    Default, 66
    Magnetic, 67
    Polygonal, 66–71, 104
Layer Style dialog box, 228–232
Layer Styles, 207–208
layers
    adding mask to, 222–223
    adjustment
        adding, 151–154
        blending using, 192–193
        retouching use of, 151–154
    centering of, 175
    Extruded Text, 300
    grouping, 153
    loading files into, 55–56
    masking, 181–183
    scaling of, 178
Layers panel, 103, 107, 140, 161–162, 222
Lens Correction dialog box, 169
lesson files
    accessing, 5
    loading, 5
lighting
    adding, 208–213
    adjusting, 210–211
    depth of field, 212–213
    sunlight, 211–212
    3D objects, 306–307
loading files into layers, 55–56

locked files, 44
logo as vector object, 237–240
Luminance, 205

M

Mac OS, 2–3, 6
Magic Wand tool, 78–80
Magnetic Lasso tool, 67
masking layers, 181–183
masks
    adding to layer, 222–223
    feathering the, 72
    in Smart Object, 206–207
Matting, 255
menu items
    editing, 22
    showing all, 22
meshes, 296, 313
metadata
    creating, 42–45
    keywords, 45–46
    locating, 42–45
    template, creating, 47–48
Metadata (Bridge), 35
Metadata panel, 43
Metallic option, Properties panel, 210
Microsoft Windows, 2–3
midtones, adjusting, 130–131
Minus sign button, 52
Missing Profile warning, 4
Move tool, 24, 26–27, 151, 157–158,
    167, 175–176, 179, 212–213, 227,
    234, 266, 301–302, 304
My Shortcuts file, 21

N

navigation
    speeding up, 10
    tips for, 11
Navigator panel
    using, 13–16
    view control using, 13
neutrals
    balancing, in image, 131–134
    definition of, 120, 124, 143
New Layer dialog box, 185
New Snapshot dialog box, 282
New Workspace dialog box, 29

O

Oil Paint
    options, 201–202
    as Smart Filter, 200
Opacity, 157
OpenGL, 296
OpenType fonts, 215
optimizing graphics for on-screen
    presentation, 244
Options bar, 79
Output values, 160

P

padlock icon, 264
Paint Brush tool, 135, 159
painting
    3D objects, 312–313
    tools for, 146
panels
    Actions, 281, 291

Preview the Optimized Image in a
    Browser button, 254
primitives, 296–298
Properties panel, 72, 220–221, 308
Properties Preset drop-down menu, 152
proxy view, 13

Q

Quick Mask, 81–83
Quick Mask mode, 81
Quick Selection tool, 73–76

R

rasterized vector text, 224
Rectangle tool, 233
Rectangular Marquee tool, 61, 108
Refine Edge dialog box, 74–75, 77
Refine Edge features, 73, 148
Refine Radius tool, 75
refining selection, 74–76
removing, 190–195
Rename button, 53
rendering, 310
resetting preferences, 3–4
resources, 6
retouching
    Clone Stamp tool for, 162–168
    example of, 156–160
    images
        adjustment layer, adding, 151–154
        new layer created from selection,
            149–151
        overview of, 146–149
        vector mask, 155

RGB color mode
    description of, 121
    highlight, 125, 128–129
    locating white and black point,
        126–127
    shadow, 125, 128–129
    working in, 122–125
Rotate the 3D Object, 303
rulers, 23–24

S

Saturation, 205
Save As dialog box, 112, 117, 147, 200
Save As dialog field, 88
Save for Web feature, 251
Save Path dialog box, 100
saving
    files for use outside of Photoshop,
        241
    keyboard shortcuts, 20–21
    paths, 100–101
    selection, 63
scaling layers, 178
screen modes, 14–15
Scrubby Zoom button, 12
searching for files
    Filter panel, 50–52
    by name or keyword, 48–50
selection(s)
    building, 61–66
    combining, 64–66
    Elliptical Marquee tool, 61
    new layer created from, 149–151
    paths added as, 101–103

Quick Mask for cleaning up, 81–83
Rectangular Marquee tool, 61, 108
refining, 74–76
saving, 63
second, transforming to create, 63–64
Smart filter, 104
tools for, 60–61, 71
transforming, 62–64
Unsharp mask applied to, 105–107
Selection tool (Illustrator), 239
Set Black Point tool, 125
Set White Point tool, 125
shadow
defining, 128–129
drop, 230–232
setting, 125
Shape drop-down menu, 233
sharpening images, 138–142
Shift+Alt/Option key, 70–71
shortcuts
creating, 17–21, 290–291
Elliptical Marquee tool, 61
navigational, 11
saving, 20–21
using, 19
Shortcuts For menu, 17
Show All Menu Items, 22
simple action, 280–282
slicing images, 273–277
Smart filter selection, 104
Smart Filters
Camera Raw as, 204–207
compositions, 140, 174–176
deleting, 204

Oil Paint as, 200
power of, 203
Smart Objects
Background layer, 104
mask used in, 206–207
using, 174–179, 197
Smart Radius, 77
special effects
Layer Styles, 207–208
lighting, 208–213
Swash characters, 215
text, 213–215
specular highlights, 125
Spellchecker dialog box, 19
Sponge tool, 166
Spot, 209
square textures, 311
stacking images, 42
Standard Screen mode, 14, 16
starting, 2–3
stereolithography files, 313
stroke added to text, 228–229
Stylization option, Oil Paint, 201
Summarize button, 21
sunlight, 211–212
Swash characters, 215
system requirements, 2

T

Tab key, 11
templates, metadata, 47–48
text
aligning, guides and grids used for,
26–27

extruded, 310
special effects, 213–215
3D, 300–301
vector
  adding, 224–228
  converting to path, 227–228
  drop shadow added to, 230–232
  rasterized, 224
  saving of, for use outside of
      Photoshop, 241
  stroke added to, 228–229
Texture option, Properties panel, 211
textures, 311–312
3D Axis, 303
3D camera tools, 301–303
3D content, downloading, 313–314
3D objects
  appearance of, 306–310
  creating, 296–301
  custom meshes, 313
  extruding paths, 298–299
  lighting, 306–307
  painting, 312–313
  primitives, 296–298
  production workflows, 313–314
  rendering, 310
  textures, 311–312
  tools, 303–306
  transforming, 301–306
  viewing, 301–306
3D text, 300–301
Threshold dialog box, 126–127
Thumbnail Grid button, 35
thumbnails, 39

tools
  Artboard, 239
  Brush, 109, 183, 190, 203
  Burn, 166
  Clone Stamp
    copying using, 185–187
    retouching using, 162–168
  Color Sampler, 127
  Crop, 147, 248
  Custom Shape, 298
  Default Lasso, 66
  Dodge, 166
  Elliptical Marquee, 61
  Erase refinement, 75
  Eyedropper, 127
  Gradient, 223, 271
  Lasso
    Default, 66
    Magnetic, 67
    Polygonal, 66–71, 104
  Magic Wand, 78–80
  Magnetic Lasso, 67
  Move, 24, 26–27, 151, 157–158, 167,
      175–176, 179, 212–213, 227,
      234, 266, 301–302, 304
  Paint Brush, 135, 159
  Path Selection, 218, 227
  Pen. *See* Pen tool
  Polygonal Lasso, 66–71, 104
  Quick Selection, 73–76
  Rectangle, 233
  Rectangular Marquee, 61, 108
  Refine Radius, 75
  selection, 60–61

white Point eyedropper tool, 129

workspaces

   Adobe Bridge, 37

   customizing, 29–30

   deleting, 30

   editing menu items from, 22

X

XML file, Image Processor settings
     saved as, 54

XMP (Extensible Metadata Platform), 43

Z

Zoom In, 11

Zoom Out, 11

Zoom tool, 12, 89, 96, 158, 164

zooming, 11–12

John Wiley & Sons, Inc.
End-User License Agreement

READ THIS. You should carefully read these terms and conditions before opening the software packet(s) included with this book "Book". This is a license agreement "Agreement" between you and John Wiley & Sons, Inc. "WILEY". By opening the accompanying software packet(s), you acknowledge that you have read and accept the following terms and conditions. If you do not agree and do not want to be bound by such terms and conditions, promptly return the Book and the unopened software packet(s) to the place you obtained them for a full refund.

1. **License Grant**. WILEY grants to you (either an individual or entity) a nonexclusive license to use one copy of the enclosed software program(s) (collectively, the "Software") solely for your own personal or business purposes on a single computer (whether a standard computer or a workstation component of a multi-user network). The Software is in use on a computer when it is loaded into temporary memory (RAM) or installed into permanent memory (hard disk, CD-ROM, or other storage device). WILEY reserves all rights not expressly granted herein.

2. **Ownership.** WILEY is the owner of all right, title, and interest, including copyright, in and to the compilation of the Software recorded on the physical packet included with this Book "Software Media". Copyright to the individual programs recorded on the Software Media is owned by the author or other authorized copyright owner of each program. Ownership of the Software and all proprietary rights relating thereto remain with WILEY and its licensers.

3. **Restrictions on Use and Transfer.**

   (a) You may only (i) make one copy of the Software for backup or archival purposes, or (ii) transfer the Software to a single hard disk, provided that you keep the original for backup or archival purposes. You may not (i) rent or lease the Software, (ii) copy or reproduce the Software through a LAN or other network system or through any computer subscriber system or bulletin-board system, or (iii) modify, adapt, or create derivative works based on the Software.

   (b) You may not reverse engineer, decompile, or disassemble the Software. You may transfer the Software and user documentation on a permanent basis, provided that the transferee agrees to accept the terms and conditions of this Agreement and you retain no copies. If the Software is an update or has been updated, any transfer must include the most recent update and all prior versions.

4. **Restrictions on Use of Individual Programs.** You must follow the individual requirements and restrictions detailed for each individual program in the "About the CD" appendix of this Book or on the Software Media. These limitations are also contained in the individual license agreements recorded on the Software Media. These limitations may include a requirement that after using the program for a specified period of time, the user must pay a registration fee or discontinue use. By opening the Software packet(s), you agree to abide by the licenses and restrictions for these individual programs that are detailed in the "About the CD" appendix and/or on the Software Media. None of the material on this Software Media or listed in this Book may ever be redistributed, in original or modified form, for commercial purposes.

Register your Digital Classroom book for exclusive benefits

Registered owners receive access to:

 The most current lesson files

 Technical resources and customer support

 Notifications of updates

 Online access to video tutorials

 Downloadable lesson files

Samples from other Digital Classroom books

Register at *DigitalClassroomBooks.com/CC/AdvPhotoshop*

DigitalClassroom

Register your book today at
DigitalClassroomBooks.com/CC/AdvPhotoshop

Office

InDesign

Illustrator

THE WAY YOU WANT TO LEARN.

HTML

Photoshop

DigitalClassroom.com

Flexible, fast, and fun, DigitalClassroom.com lets you choose when, where, and how to learn new skills. This subscription-based online learning environment is accessible anytime from your desktop, laptop, tablet, or smartphone. It's easy, efficient learning — on *your* schedule.

- Learn web design and development, Office applications, and new technologies from more than 2,500 video tutorials, e-books, and lesson files
- Master software from Adobe, Apple, and Microsoft
- Interact with other students in forums and groups led by industry pros

Learn more! Sample DigitalClassroom.com for free, now!

We're social. Connect with us!

facebook.com/digitalclassroom
@digitalclassrm